Battleground Europe
NORMANDY

OMAHA BEACH
V Corps Battle for the Beachhead

With the continued expansion of the Battleground series a **Battleground Europe Club** has been formed to benefit the reader. The purpose of the Club is to keep members informed of new titles and key developments by way of a quarterly newsletter, and to offer many other reader-benefits. Membership is free and by registering an interest you can help us predict print runs and thus maintain prices at their present levels. Please call the office 01226 734555, or send your name and address along with a request for more information to:
Battleground Europe Club
Pen & Sword Books Ltd, 47 Church Street, Barnsley, South Yorkshire S70 2AS

Battleground Europe
NORMANDY

OMAHA BEACH
V CORPS BATTLE FOR THE BEACHHEAD

Tim Kilvert-Jones

LEO COOPER

COMBINED PUBLISHING
Pennsylvania

Published by
LEO COOPER
an imprint of
Pen & Sword Books Limited
47 Church Street, Barnsley, South Yorkshire S70 2AS
Copyright © Tim Kilvert-Jones, 1999

ISBN 0 85052 671 X

A CIP catalogue of this book is available
from the British Library

Printed by Redwood Books Limited
Trowbridge, Wiltshire

*For up-to-date information on other titles produced under the Leo Cooper
imprint, please telephone or write to:*
Pen & Sword Books Ltd, FREEPOST, 47 Church Street
Barnsley, South Yorkshire S70 2AS
Telephone 01226 734222

Published under licence in the United States of America by

COMBINED PUBLISHING

ISBN 1-58097-015-X

For information, address:
COMBINED PUBLISHING
P.O. Box 307
Conshohocken, PA 19428
E-Mail: combined@dca.net
Web: www.combinedpublishing.com
Orders: 1-800-418-6065

*Cataloguing in Publication Data available from the Library of
Congress*

CONTENTS

Cover painting: *Omaha Beach* by George Sottung (1979) by kind permission of the
United States Coastguard Academy.

FOREWORD
by

COLONEL BILL FRIEDMAN US ARMY (Retd.)
S-1, 16th Infantry Regiment,
1st Infantry Division, Omaha Beach

This book could only have been written by a soldier. A soldier with a wide strategic vision and sense of order, because war is inherently incoherent and needs explanation – Tim Kilvert-Jones provides this. A Sandhurst graduate, he is a former regular army officer in the British Army with a long and diverse service including the Falklands, Northern Ireland, the Middle East and Haiti. As a consequence he sees the theatre, the battlefield and ground-eye view of the terrain that is the infantryman's, and presents these factors for the reader to assimilate. Tim is now an internationally-recognized military analyst and strategist in the United States.

For one so intimately associated with the assault landing, my experience was confined to a few yards of beach – at least for the first two hours. Along with the thousands of men escaping from the assault landing craft, I laid immobile behind the largely imagined protection of the famous shingle ledge at the beach's high water mark. All I could see was a long line of men taking cover each side of me and a bluff to my front. I really had no desire to see more. As for understanding or appreciating the great forces, Herculean efforts, good and bad guesses, brilliant strategies (and there were those too), unit and individual actions, and the astronomical number of interrelated events, I had not the foggiest. Only now am I beginning to comprehend the enormity of D-Day.

I went ashore at 0810 hours as part of the 16th Infantry Regimental Command Party, Colonel George C. Taylor commanding. Colonel Taylor was a much beloved man in the whole sense. I was then the Regimental Adjutant charged with personnel and administrative matters.

The 16th Infantry Regiment was, and still is, very dear to me. It was the Regiment I joined after receiving my regular army commission in 1941 and I stayed with it until the breaching of the Siegfried Line at Aachen, Germany, in the fall of 1944.

I give unstinting credit to the raw courage and gallantry of the members of the 115th and 116th Infantry Regiments of the 29th

Bill Friedman (third from right) talking to President Clinton on the 50th Anniversary.

Division; to each and every gunner on the warships that covered our advance; to the coxswains who carried us ashore; to the Rangers of legendary strength and tenacity; and to the thousands of soldiers, sailors and airmen of all ranks, nationalities and skills who made our lodgement in Normandy possible. But, as I see it, it was the beautiful, wild, to hell-with-you 16th that did it at Omaha. Its soldiers walked through the minefields, took out German fortifications and seized the bluffs. I shall always feel humble in the light of what I personally know the heroes of the 16th accomplished on that surreal day in June 1944.

Tim Kilvert-Jones is to be commended for recognizing a very special friend of the First Division, and particularly the 16th Infantry, Bob Capa. Capa was certainly one of the finest, gutsiest war photographers who ever walked on a battlefield. He had an incredible feel for what war looked like and how it could be captured on film. We became good friends in Africa and before we embarked to France he called me and asked if I could get him a billet with the 16th. Colonel Taylor agreed and he went ashore with our Company E. I was devastated by the news of his death in Vietnam years later.

Thanks to Tim Kilvert-Jones for allowing future generations to see 'Bloody Omaha' as it was on 6 June, 1944.

We owe you!

7

INTRODUCTION

Understanding Historic Battlefields

The focus of the guidebook will be on one short, momentous, but bloody event in the mid-20th century, the assault by a joint military force from the United States of America on a German-defended and fortified sector of the Normandy coastline on 6th June 1944.

This book has application for the interested tourist, military historian and the contemporary serviceman. It offers both itineraries and background materials that will be of value to either the studious, or simply the curious. This is a self-contained guide for the battlefield visitor. It has been written to facilitate tours and studies of the events in the Omaha sector of the Operation Neptune-Overlord lodgement area.

An appreciation of the military framework behind the operations of V Corps and the Rangers in the Omaha sector on 6th June 1944 is a fundamental necessity. In order to appreciate the scale of this battlefield and the significance of the great sacrifice made by so many young men in the assault divisions of June 1944, it is essential to visualize the whole 'canvas' of Operation Neptune-Overlord. To that end Chapter 1 will provide sufficient explanation for the reader to fit the more personal accounts of battle into what Winston Churchill described thus: 'this vast operation is undoubtedly the most complicated and difficult that has ever occurred.'

The specific combat actions that are discussed in this book occurred at the tactical level. The tactical level of war is concerned with the conduct of battles and engagements; these normally unfold within a sequence of major operations. Above this level of military activity lies the operational level of conflict. This level provides the gearing between national political and military strategy and all tactical activities in a theatre of operations. It is at the operational level that military resources are directed to achieve the campaign objectives, or end-state. In Normandy, the operational commander was General Dwight D. Eisenhower, the Supreme Allied Commander. Eisenhower arrived in London in January 1944 to take up an appointment that would influence the very conduct of the Anglo-American effort against Germany. He was not operating in a vacuum. Eisenhower received strategic guidance from the political leaders of the western powers principally President Roosevelt of the United States and Prime Minister Winston Churchill in Britain.

Military direction was then issued by either the Joint Chiefs, or via the national military strategic authorities; in Washington D.C. General George Marshall spoke for the President, while in London, General Alan Brooke spoke for Churchill.

Visiting Normandy

Normandy is a region steeped in a rich blend of history and culture. The quiet villages, verdant countryside, dramatic castles, memorials and museums present physical evidence of an Anglo-Saxon, Viking, Norman, French, and English heritage. That dynamic blend of cultures is characterized by an inscription on the Commonwealth Memorial to the Missing in Bayeux. It reads:

'We, once conquered by William, have now set free the Conqueror's native land.'

D-Day in Perspective

D-Day was the greatest combined amphibious assault the world has yet seen. It was a staggering feat of planning and synchronized military action. On that day a total of 176,475 men, 3,000 guns, 1,500 tanks and 15,000 other assorted vehicles landed in Normandy across the assault beaches or by glider and parachute onto the fields of France. In all, eight Allied divisions were put ashore. They then pressed back the remnants of the German coastal defence units already battered by days of bombardment and then bloodied at close quarters on 6th June. This extraordinary summary of achievement belies the very real fear, exhilaration, cost and horror endured by those men and women touched by this climactic battle.

Hours before the assault forces had even reached France, Eisenhower had actually prepared a message to the Allied Chiefs of Staff in the event of failure. The unsent message ordered a complete re-embarkation from Normandy because 'the venture has been overtaken by misfortune amounting to a disaster.' His note concluded with 'If any blame or fault attaches to the attempt it is mine alone.' Over-shadowed by grim memories of Gallipoli and Dieppe, Churchill also privately feared for the outcome of this decisive battle and expected Allied losses to reach 20,000 men amongst the leading assault divisions.

On 6th June 1944 disaster would only really threaten the Allies at Omaha Beach. Here the V US Corps launched its Rangers, elements of the 29th 'Blue and Gray' Division under command of the veteran

9

'Big Red One' (1st Division), in a frontal assault against a natural, well defended, fortress between Pointe du Hoc and St. Honorine. That the operation was to prove successful is a testament to the undaunted courage and small unit leadership of so many young men throughout the Omaha assault force.

In close support of the tank troopers, engineers, infantrymen, sailors and coastguardsmen were the surface combatants of the United States and Royal Navies. Of particular note in this study will be the vital contribution made by the eight destroyers of Destroyer Squadron (DESRON) 18 and their three attached British vessels. These destroyers had a fundamental part in the successful outcome of the battle for the beachhead. Their intimate support of the American soldiers caught in German killing areas on Omaha Beach and at Pointe du Hoc in the early morning of 6th June would prove decisive in making the subsequent, though bloody, victory possible.

The terrible events of that Tuesday morning in June 1944 have earned this beach the sobriquet 'Bloody Omaha.' After three days of fighting in the Omaha and Utah beachheads, over 4,000 American soldiers from the 1st, 2nd, 4th, and 29th Divisions would be casualties; over 3,500 of those casualties fell at, or just beyond, Omaha Beach. In addition, three destroyers, a destroyer escort, a heavily laden troopship, and numerous other assault craft would be lost off the two American First Army beaches. This would prove to be a ferocious and brutal battle.

Today, Omaha's 7,000 yards of golden sands, cliffs and rolling escarpment bear the poignant memorials of war. Parts of the storm destroyed Mulberry Harbour can still be seen, both on the beach and integrated into the Vierville fisherman's pier. The beautiful Normandy American National Military Cemetery at St. Laurent also overlooks the sands and salt marsh where so many young men faced their greatest test of individual and collective courage. The cemetery and its paths will form a focal point for any visit to the area and it is described in detail in the Appendices. To the West of Omaha lies Pointe du Hoc with its preserved, yet still scarred and cratered landscape, shattered bunkers and deep fortifications. There the sheer 100-foot cliffs still leave one breathless at the courage of Colonel Rudder and his Rangers.

Learning from Experience

As a tool of professional education, the study of military history cannot provide universal remedies for today's soldiers; as Napoleon stated: 'what is good in one case is bad in another.' However, in peace the serviceman can gain some vicarious experience from the effective study of military history. Today, the battlefields of Normandy offer the student and soldier alike a poignant reminder of the realities of war. The complex and relatively unchanged terrain, the well-documented German defences, the detailed force ratios and now the declassified, intricate planning processes, all make this battlefield an excellent 'schoolhouse' for the study of operational art and specific tactical techniques and procedures. For the soldier or serious student, there is no doubt that a little preparatory work will be rewarded by a more valuable visit to the Normandy coast.

Throughout this study, it is worth remembering that the Normandy campaign offers an excellent example of contrasting military cultures and capabilities. On D-Day, the Allies enjoyed complete air superiority and naval dominance. This dominant capability allowed the assaulting armies and corps to exploit the synergy inherent in highly trained and thoroughly rehearsed joint and combined forces. This dynamic and powerful force was

A sight common along the south coast of England. American troops preparing to embark for Normandy from 'somewhere in England'.

unleashed against an enemy that could do little more than fight a series of uncoordinated, independent and frequently isolated actions. Yet even with such a disadvantage, the combination of simple coastal defences covered by effective weapons in the hands of experienced, well-sited and well-equipped German soldiers on dominating terrain proved devastating to the initial waves of young men thrown up against Hitler's fabled Fortress Europe.

Other factors contributed to the near disaster at Omaha Beach, including the loss of much of the amphibious supporting armour and artillery in the rough seas. The weather also hampered air operations. Because of the cloud conditions in the early morning of 6th June, several preplanned air strikes by American bombers proved to be wholly ineffective. Fearful of 'dropping short' onto the assault boats during their final run-in, the bombers dropped their devastating payloads beyond the beach, behind the German defences. Some disruption to communications may have occurred but in essence the troops on the bluffs, who were well-sited to counter an amphibious assault, were left relatively unscathed.

Rear Admiral John L. Hall USN identified further problems after the battle. He acknowledged that the 40-minute naval preparatory bombardment had been too short to disrupt, destroy or even adequately demoralize the defenders. The strong lateral current at Omaha Beach would also hamper navigation. Many of the unseaworthy assault landing craft drifted into other units' objective areas during the run-in. Navigating officers were hampered by smoke, enemy fire and the German beach obstacles sited below the high water mark. As a result, many of the assault troops would find themselves approaching an unfamiliar sector of the beach, frequently directly into the face of alert, powerful German strongpoints.

The Tours

This book will guide the reader, whether student, veteran, or soldier through the initial battle for the V Corps beachhead. Events from the early stages of planning Operation Neptune, through to the battles on 6th June 1944 will be examined. This book contains two specific tours:

Tour A: Pointe du Hoc and the assault by the Rangers on 6th June 1944

Tour B: Omaha Beach and the assault by V US Corps on 6th June

1944. This is divided into two parts:

Tour B-1: 29th Division 's battle for the beachhead in the west.

Tour B-2: 1st Division's assault at the eastern end of Omaha Beach.

These sequential tours can be completed within a day if transport is used whenever possible, to move between the various locations. Alternatively the tours can be taken at a more leisurely pace. The serious explorer may wish to intersperse studies of the battlefield with visits to appropriate museums, military cemeteries or other associated sites of interest. In that case at least two days should be set aside to get the most out of the story of Omaha Beach and its environs. If the visitor wishes to sample the gastronomic delights of the region, or visit the many other sites of interest within a short drive of the landing beaches, then a full week should be set aside for the exploration of this rich 'department' of northern France.

The robust walking explorer will find that there is now a coastal path known locally as the 'Sentier Littoral' from Grandcamp Maisy, Pointe du Hoc , via Omaha Beach, to the St. Laurent cemetery. The path is well marked and takes the walker on a 10-mile hike along the coast and across the cliff tops. It has been sited by the *Conservatoire du Littoral* (Coast Conservation Trust) to take walkers through many of the key sites referred to in this book. The complete walk or part thereof, is spectacular in fine weather. Please bear in mind that it is useful to have transportation at the far end otherwise time and effort will be lost on the return leg of the journey.

Each tour is accompanied by a historical account; these accounts should be used as background materials to the more poignant study of the ground, the memorials and the personal memories of the men who fought in the Omaha sector. In addition to these suggested tours, this book provides the reader with selected recommendations for visits to associated sites of general interest within the Lodgment Area. Today, there is no shortage of private museums and memorials competing, along with the more significant national and regional collections, for the visitors' attention and revenue. The visitor to Normandy needs to choose carefully and so leave these hallowed fields feeling fulfilled rather than frustrated.

D-Day and the Battle for Normandy remain amongst the most fascinating and accessible European military campaigns in the long, painful history of human conflict. Since the end of World War II, the region's military history has attracted a broad range of pilgrims. The veterans and their families have been frequent, if unwitting

13

Landing craft assembled at Southampton in readiness for the invasion of Europe.

companions to historians and soldiers studying this momentous campaign. Whether you will be playing on the beautiful beaches or touring across the open fields beyond the dunes into the bocage, you cannot avoid the evidence of great sacrifice, terrible loss and the glory that surrounds this now beautiful, tranquil and ancient region of France.

What to Take

The weather in Normandy can be fickle throughout the year. Be prepared to face the hazards of sun or rain. Stout walking boots are advisable if the visitor intends to leave the well-marked paths. A waterproof jacket is also essential. The additional tools of the battlefield tourist are also recommended: a light portable stool or shooting stick, binoculars, camera, and this guidebook, of course! Michelin maps are an excellent and essential aid to navigation. The following maps are a useful start point and can usually be obtained from most well stocked book shops in France and Britain:

Carte Topographique. Institut Geographique National (IGN) Number 6: Caen-Cherbourg 1:100,000. If visits will be made to the eastern extremities of the invasion area, then IGN map Number 7 will also be required. This map covers an area from Ouistreham in the West, across the Orne River and its ship canal, where Pegasus Bridge can be found, and so onto the northeast, Merville Battery and beyond.

Other useful maps include Michelin's map Number 54 'Normandie' in the 1:200,000 series, which covers the whole invasion area, but at a considerably smaller scale.

The serious student or walker may also acquire appropriate maps from the IGN 1:50,000 series in order to find the more obscure routes through the region.

Military students are advised to obtain copies of the excellent French military map series available through official map acquisition processes within their formation headquarters.

Copies of original Allied planning and battle maps for Neptune-Overlord are available from the Imperial War Museum, London.

ACKNOWLEDGMENTS

Stephen Ambrose in *Citizen Soldiers* wrote, 'Normandy was a soldier's battle. It belonged to the riflemen, machine gunners, mortarmen, tankers, and artillerymen who were on the front lines...There was a simplicity to the fighting: for the Germans, to hold; for the Americans, to attack.' He was right. In the research for this book I had the honour and privilege of interviewing a number of those very special veterans from V Corps at Omaha Beach. I owe my gratitude to every one of these venerable gentlemen who gave so much of their youth and souls in the name of freedom and the service of their great nation.

I owe particular thanks to Bill Friedman, a true gentleman, warrior, 'Europhile' and an undoubted hero in his own right. He opened my eyes to the realities of a battle that has been simplified and misjudged by academics and historians over time. His own record of service to the United States of America would make a book in itself. His extraction from Aachen in late 1944 at the request of his widowed mother and at the orders of General George C. Marshall is also worthy of a screenplay or film.

I also wish to thank Blythe Foote Finke. Blythe is the widow of John Finke who argued up to his death with Joe Dawson, as to who got to the top of the bluffs first. Blythe captured the recollections of her husband and his friends and fellow veterans of Omaha Beach in an excellent book, *No Mission Too Difficult*, a selective oral history of the 1st Division in World War II. I wish to also thank Gerald Griffin, Ray Lambert, Dick Cole, Fred Hall, John Bentz Carroll; each and every one of them are representative of the brave, though often unassuming men, who fought across that bloody beach in the name of liberation and freedom. We owe them all so very much.

I also wish to acknowledge the contribution made by the Association of the 16th Infantry Regiment and John Votaw and the First Division Museum at Cantigny. The US Navy Museum and the historical branch of the US Coast Guard, both in Washington D.C., also provided excellent assistance in the research of this work.

Finally, I must express my gratitude to Professor Williamson Murray of the Army War College at Carlisle, Pennsylvania, and his colleague and former student Dr. Russell Hart, senior Lecturer in the Department of History at Ohio State University. Dr. Hart gave me full access to his eminent but as yet unpublished dissertation on the battle for Normandy.

My wife Louise and our children, Edward, Victoria and Hugo must also be thanked for their patience and tolerance of a husband and father too often confined to his study to meet his publisher's deadline.

Any errors or lack of acknowledgement are the author's fault alone. This book has been written in honour of the veterans who fought in Normandy and for whom there can have been few greater tests than crossing the fire-raked sands at Omaha Beach or scaling the near vertical cliffs at Pointe du Hoc. On June 6th, 1944 they were a very long way from their homes in the New World.

TD Kilvert-Jones   May 1999
Fairfax, Virginia
tkilve5070@aol.com

US Army in Britain rehearse invasion tactics. Assault troops wade ashore in support during an attack on the 'enemy occupied' beach.

CHAPTER ONE

THE SECOND FRONT

By the winter of 1943 the Germans were already engaged in a multi-front war. In the east, the finest units of the Wehrmacht and Waffen SS were being consumed at an appalling rate. In the Mediterranean, the Axis powers had been defeated in North Africa, an Anglo-American expeditionary force had conquered Sicily and the mainland of Italy had now been invaded. In the skies over Germany an air war of extraordinary proportions was also consuming manpower and industrial production capacity as losses of aircraft and ground defences climbed. In an effort to stem the devastating tide of day and night area bombing by the Allied bomber fleets, the Germans relocated fighter wings and air defence systems to protect the Fatherland at the cost of other fronts. The German air defence system (including searchlight units, gun crews, and radar centres) had absorbed 900,000 men alone. All these assets were being employed well away from what was to be the decisive 'Second Front'.

Defending the Reich: Fortress Europe

In December 1941 Adolf Hitler ordered his national military command headquarters, the Oberkommando der Wehrmacht, to plan 'the construction of a new West Wall to assure protection of the Arctic, North Sea and Atlantic coasts... against any landing operation of very considerable strength with the employment of the smallest number of static forces.' On 23 March 1942, with the Third Reich at the peak of its success, he went on to issue his Führer Directive Number 40. This directive set down the detailed defensive responsibilities for the operational commanders in the West. It stated:

> 'The coastline of Europe will, in the coming months, be exposed to the danger of the enemy landing in force... Even enemy landings with limited objectives can interfere seriously with our own plans if they result in the enemy gaining any kind of foothold on the coast... Enemy forces that have landed must be destroyed or thrown back into the sea by immediate counterattack.'

Ironically three days after he had signed this directive the British

17

mounted the highly successful though costly raid on the port and dry dock facilities at St. Nazaire. The raid was so effective that the 'Normandie' dry dock (destroyed by the explosive laden HMS *Campbletown*) was inoperable for the rest of the war. Within five months, on 19 August, the German defences were further probed by Operation Jubilee, the disastrous raid at Dieppe. This operation was a frontal assault on a partly fortified harbour. The German defenders used their limited fortifications and counter-attack troops to devastating effect. After 9 hours the Anglo-Canadian force withdrew leaving behind 3,658 men out of the 5,100 troops who had landed. One thousand men had been killed and the remainder were either wounded, missing or taken prisoner. The Germans had suffered 300 casualties. The costly experience at Dieppe was to provide diverse lessons that would be fundamental to the subsequent successful landings in North Africa, Sicily in 1943 and in Normandy one year later.

For the most part the German newspaper headlines in late August 1942 illustrated the Führer's sentiments on Jubilee: 'Catastrophic Defeat a Setback to Invasion...What does Stalin say about this Disaster to Churchill's Invasion?' For the Reich, the Allied disaster provided valuable propaganda material and a reassurance that lightly held fortified defences could repel enemy amphibious assaults. The Germans certainly viewed the Anglo-Canadian operation as an amateurish undertaking. They were right.

Work on the West Wall (also known as the Atlantic Wall) now began in earnest amid a blaze of propaganda. The focus of effort was on the major ports (the evident target of enemy raids and any future invasion) and then on vulnerable coastal areas, such as the Pas de Calais, Hook of Holland and the Gironde estuary. The Germans had once again forgotten their own history; it was Frederick the Great of Prussia who had stated 'He who defends everything, defends nothing.' In reality, what emerged was a loose necklace of powerful fortresses such as Calais and Cherbourg, interconnected by weak outposts and routine patrol activities spread over 2400 miles of coastline. Inflexible dogma and self-delusion had replaced effective critical analysis of the threat now gathering strength across the Channel.

The Germans were also hampered by shortages of defensive materials such as concrete, mines, adequate weapons, fighting men and labour. By 1943 the war in the East was draining the Reich's increasingly limited resources. The manpower shortfall was

Success: The commando attack on the dry dock at St Nazaire in 1942. The installation was destroyed when the *Campbeltown* slammed into the dock gate and later exploded.

Failure: the disastrous raid at Dieppe. This operation was a frontal assault on a partly fortified harbour. After 9 hours the Anglo-Canadian force withdrew leaving behind 3,658 men out of the 5,100 troops who had landed.

identified by Commander-in-Chief West , Field Marshal Gerd Von Rundstedt. He reported in October 1943, that the existing Wall could be 'covered' but not fully defended. Yet he also recognized the utility of the Wall as a propaganda tool and, to a lesser extent, the military value of Hitler 's port-city fortress policy. That policy would actually lead to the denial or destruction of the principal French ports in the face of the Allied advance for several months after D-Day. However, Von Rundstedt went on to note that:

Field Marshal Gerd Von Rundstedt

'A rigid German defence [is] impossible there for any length of time, the outcome of the battle must depend on the use of a mobile and armoured reserve... the best that might be hoped for [is] that it might hold up an attack for twenty four hours, but any resolute assault [is] bound to make a breakthrough anywhere along it in a day at most. And once through all the rest could be taken from the rear...'

Führer Directive Number 51

On 3rd November 1943 Hitler issued one of the half dozen of his most significant directives of the war. Führer Directive N. 51 specified the tasks required of OB West to create an effective bastion against an Anglo-American landing. The Directive stated:

'... If the enemy here succeeds in penetrating our defences on a wide front, consequences of staggering proportions will follow within a short time. All signs point to an offensive in the Western Front no later than spring, and perhaps earlier.

For that reason I can no longer justify the further weakening of the West in favour of other theatres of war. I have therefore decided to strengthen the defences in the West, particularly at places from which we shall launch our long-range

Adolf Hitler

war against England. For those are the very points at which the enemy must and will attack: there – unless all indications are misleading – will be fought the decisive invasion battle.'

Hitler went on to issue specific tasks to the Army, Luftwaffe, Navy, and SS and closed with a warning: 'All authorities will guard against wasting time and energy in useless jurisdictional squabbles, and will direct all their efforts toward strengthening our defensive and offensive power.' Fortunately for the Allies, Hitler's subordinate component commanders and even individual Arms commanders ignored this final demand. That divisive situation would be further exacerbated by his imposition of a complex, contradictory, and ineffective command structure on his forces in the West.

Arrival of Rommel in the West: December 1943

By 5th November 1943 Hitler had promulgated his new Führer Directive and selected Rommel as his Inspector General of Defences in the West. By the end of the month Rommel had gathered about him a specialist joint staff to support his analysis of the West Wall. He moved from Italy to France with his own Army Group B Headquarters and quickly set about a gruelling programme of inspections from Denmark to the Spanish border. He focused much of his effort on the most likely areas for the impending invasion: Pas de Calais, the Somme estuary, Normandy, including the Cotentin, Peninsula, Brittany, and the Netherlands.

As a result of Rommel's highly critical report and recommendations, Hitler decided to incorporate Army Group B into OB West on 31st December. Rommel now found himself under Von Rundstedt's command, with specific responsibility for anti-invasion plans from the Netherlands and across northern France. His command was divided into the Seventh Army West of the River Orne, and Fifteenth Army to its East, with the 88th Corps in Holland.

Rommel assessed that to have any hope of success 'the enemy must be annihilated before he reaches our main battle line,' therefore 'we must stop him in the water.' Rommel ordered the laying of 200 million mines along the coast to form an initial barrier. Between November 1943 and mid-May 1944 over half a million anti-invasion obstacles were put in place along with a total of 4 million mines. One month before the invasion he was able to report 'I am more

Hitler selected Rommel as his Inspector General of Defences in the West. Here the Field Marshal is seen having the finer points of a of beach obstacle explained to him.

confident than ever before. If the British give us just two more weeks, I won't have any more doubt about it.'

The frenetic preparatory activity throughout Army Group B was a major concern to the Allies. In fact, the Allied planners were so concerned with Rommel's beach defences that they adjusted the preferred time and conditions necessary for the amphibious assault. The seaborne invasion had been initially planned to take place under the cover of darkness, but now it would commence after first light. Better visibility would give the navy a chance to manoeuvre through the increasingly complex and lethal 'forest' of obstacles along the beaches.

German Intelligence Assessments and the Impact on Strategy

During early 1944 Rommel would bemoan his lack of knowledge of Allied intentions. He wrote 'I know nothing for certain about the enemy'. The Allied air forces were effectively preventing most German reconnaissance flights reaching the southern coast of Britain – now densely packed with shipping, men and materiel.

Rommel was strategically blind. His headquarters along with Fremde Heeres West (Foreign Armies West), the German military intelligence organization focused on establishing the strength and intentions of the Anglo-American armies in Britain, was also completely misled by 'Bodyguard', a highly effective deception plan designed to tie down many of Hitler's reserves away from the Norman coastline. On 20th March they could do little better than assess that the impending assault would occur 'somewhere between the Pas de Calais and the Loire valley'. As a result of the complex deception conducted within the Bodyguard framework of operations, the Germans believed that the Allies had 90 operational divisions in the UK (double the actual strength). They assessed that 20 of those divisions were poised to land in the first wave – four times the actual strength intended for the D-Day assault. The Germans believed that with so many divisions apparently prepared for the forthcoming invasion, the Anglo-American forces would be able to mount two expeditions in rapid succession, probably in the Pas de Calais and one other location. German assessments of this fictitious Allied capability and intent were further manipulated and reinforced by the information passed back to the Reich by German agents in Britain, most notably agent GARBO.

The Abwehr (German Military Intelligence) staff in Spain had recruited GARBO, or rather Juan Pujol Garcia, as a potential agent for operations in Britain. By the time Pujol was deployed to southern England in 1942 he had already been 'turned'. As a controlled double agent he established a fictitious network of 27 additional 'sources' located across the southern counties. GARBO then passed a web of deception back to his Abwehr controller, Karl Erich Kuhlenthal, in Spain. Kuhlenthal was so impressed with the information that he re-transmitted it to his headquarters in Berlin. The Abwehr informed GARBO: 'Your activity and that of your informants gave us a perfect idea of what is taking place over there. These reports... have an incalculable value.' Ironically the Germans were to decorate Pujol for his services to their war effort with the Iron Cross on 17th June 1944. Within months the Director General of MI5 would also award him with an MBE for his contribution to both the Bodyguard operation and the fixing of the German 15th Army in the Pas de Calais.

Blind and misled, Rommel still managed to analyze the threat and conceive of a credible defensive strategy that with hindsight and evidence from Omaha Beach, appears to have had the best chance of actually defeating or disrupting the invasion.

Any obstacle crossing or expeditionary operation is most vulnerable to counter-attack while the assaulting force is establishing its beachhead. If Rommel could hold the assault divisions on the foreshore and then launch local counter-attacks using all available armoured forces, he would stand a good chance of disrupting or defeating the invasion. Even in 1944 there was no doubt of German superiority in armour. A few panzers would have had a dramatic impact on landing operations if they could have been pre-positioned in hides close to the beaches.

The German Armoured Reserves

Rommel now sought control of the panzer forces under command of OB West. As a result of his experiences in North Africa where his Afrika Korps had been under relentless enemy air attacks in the latter phase of the North Africa campaign, Rommel recognized the need to deploy his reserves well forward. This would minimize their exposure to both air attacks and the effects of enemy air interdiction around the landing area.

But the reality was that in the absence of any effective intelligence, he would have to disperse these limited resources to cover the most likely invasion areas: from the Pas de Calais through Normandy to the Cotentin. Yet once the direction of the enemy attack had been identified he would still be able to throw the nearest panzer units into battle, if necessary piecemeal. He felt that he could afford to do this because of the qualitative advantage of the German panzers over any Allied fighting vehicle then in service. Individually, there was little doubt that German tanks were superior. They had better armour and carried more powerful weapons and were usually commanded and crewed by experienced veterans. This meant that in most engagements, each individual German tank had a qualitative and often a tactical advantage over its numerically superior enemy counterpart.

Once Rommel had codified his strategy for defeating the invasion, he sought the resources to make the concept a reality. He now demanded operational control of the panzer arm in OB West. A fundamental disagreement emerged between two divergent doctrinal camps. On the one hand Rommel believed in the forward deployment of the panzers and had some support from Hitler. On the other hand the veteran panzer commanders from the Eastern

Panzerkampfwagen Mk V (Panther). German tanks were superior; they had better armour and carried more powerful weapons and were usually commanded and crewed by experienced veterans. In most engagements each individual German tank had a qualitative and often a tactical advantage over its numerically superior opponent.

Front, such as General der Panzertruppen Geyr Von Schweppenburg, supported by Guderian (Inspector General of Panzers) and the ageing Von Rundstedt, favoured holding the panzer reserves well back from the coast until the enemy's intentions and strength became clear. At that point a well-planned and concentrated counter-attack could be launched. Rommel therefore demanded operational control of all the armoured formations in OB West. This would then allow him to site these powerful forces in forward concentration areas close to the likely invasion sites along the coastline. From their hides he would then be able to deploy them promptly and with the shortest exposure to air attack to the invasion front.

Within his concept of operations, Rommel planned to use his nearest panzer divisions as a hasty counter-attack force. While that initial action was being fought to both bolster the coastal defences and destroy localized penetrations, he would bring the more distant formations to the battle area to mount further attacks on any weakly held enemy lodgment. Those more distant divisions would need to redeploy to the new front, moving on exterior lines, and probably

being harried from the air by Allied fighter bombers operating well within range of the French coast from their British airfields. However, this exposed journey could still prove to be shorter than a move from some inland concentration area designated by the cautious Von Rundstedt, or his traditional cavalry tacticians who wanted to mass their panzer arm before delivering a 'text-book' decisive blow.

This traditional approach ignored the inherent strength of Allied air power and the ability of the Anglo-American armies to concentrate artillery and naval gunfire in devastating co-ordinated bombardments. It also fell exactly into place with General Montgomery's assessment of how the German's would conduct the defence.

General Guderian
(Inspector General of Panzers)

During his briefing to all general officers of the field armies at St. Paul's School, London on 7th April 1944, Montgomery explained that:

> *'Rommel is likely to hold his mobile divisions back from the coast until he is certain where our main effort is being made. He will concentrate them quickly and strike a hard blow, his static divisions will endeavour to hold on defensively to important ground and act as pivots to counter-attacks...'*

Unfortunately for Rommel, Von Schweppenburg commanding Panzer Group West, was headquartered in Paris close to Von Rundstedt's OB West. In 1944 he had responsibility for the training of the panzer and panzergrenadier divisions under Von Rundstedt's command. His principal staff was entirely composed of experienced panzer and grenadier officers. From Paris, Geyr also retained an element of operational control over three of the armoured divisions in theatre. His responsibilities were now to bring him into direct contact – and on occasions, conflict – with Rommel.

German Unity of Effort and Unity of Command

Fortunately for the Allies neither side won the argument. Hitler , ever suspicious of his army commanders, allowed the debate to impede any form of unified command in the West. He received a series of visitors who lobbied him in favour of one or other solutions. Guderian describes in his memoirs one such visit to gain Hitler's support for the formation of a Front Reserve. The response to this request was a long statistical summary of fortification and mining programmes conducted on the West Wall and an endorsement of the 'Rommel Doctrine' that the first 48 hours of the invasion would be critical.

Back in France, Rommel was now involved in acrimonious debates with Von Rundstedt over the location of individual divisions such as their argument over the location of the 2nd Panzer Division astride the River Somme at Abbeville. In such an atmosphere of mistrust Rommel alternated between bouts of defeatism to absolute confidence. His swings of emotion were noted and briefed to Hitler who decided to temporize. North of the River Loire, Rommel (Army Group B) was given command of 2nd, 21st and 116th Panzer Divisions. So in all, Rommel now had 39 infantry and 3 panzer divisions under his command by June 1944. Of his vital panzer formations, 21st Panzer Division was located near Caen, Sword Beach and the Orne Bridges, while 2nd Panzer Division was located in the Pas de Calais and 116th was concentrated near Paris. Meanwhile, Hitler left Von Rundstedt in command of Panzer Group West including Panzer Lehr, and 12 SS *Hitler Jugend* in accordance with OKW's recommendation. To add to this complex command structure the 12 SS Panzer and 17th SS Panzergrenadier Divisions along with 1st SS *Leibstandarte* were part of the 1st SS Panzer Corps under General 'Sepp' Dietrich. These powerful, elite forces were deployed between Brussels and Poitiers.

Ironically in Führer Directive No. 40 of 23rd March 1942, entitled 'Command Organisations on the Coasts,' Hitler had stated:

'The preparation and execution of defensive operations must unequivocally and unreservedly be concentrated in the hands of one man.'

It was fortunate for the Allies that Hitler did not follow through on his own directives. Inevitably, each layer of authority that he imposed would add new complexities and frictions to the already hardened arteries of command in OB West. To add a final measure of delay to any flexible or responsive decision-making, Hitler demanded that none of the armoured reserves could be deployed without his personal authority. Crucial hours and days would now be lost after midnight on 6th June as the army commanders awaited decisions from their distant Commander-in-Chief. Hitler had ensured that neither of his Field Marshals in the West would have decisive command over the crucial armoured reserves.

Germany's Multiple Front War

At the strategic level one must recall the Soviet contribution to D-Day. In reality, the Red Army was grinding the greater part of the German war machine to dust far away from Normandy. In 1943 at the Tehran conference, Stalin had promised to launch an offensive that would fix and destroy Hitler's ability to switch assets from Russia to France during the critical first month of the build-up in Normandy.

As June progressed, the strategic situation would deteriorate further for the Reich as Hitler became distracted by events in the East and the preparations for the expected Soviet summer offensive. Operation Bagration would annihilate Germany's Army Group Centre between 22-30th June. This Soviet offensive in western Russia had been timed to disrupt German attempts to switch reserves from the Eastern Front to meet the new threat in

In the last week of June 1944 the Soviet Union shattered the German front line in their summer offensive. Within a week the Third Reich had lost 154,000 men, either killed or taken prisoner. Over 50,000 German prisoners, their officers leading, were paraded through the streets of Moscow flanked by lines of silent citizens. Moscow's cleansing department followed with trucks swilling the roads with disinfectant.

Normandy. With over 1.7 million men supported by over 4,000 tanks and assault guns, 6,000 aircraft and 26,000 artillery or rocket systems, the Red Army shattered the German frontline. Within a week the Third Reich had lost 154,000 men, either killed or taken prisoner. Materiel losses defy imagination; in one week, 2,000 tanks, 10,000 guns, and 57,000 vehicles had been destroyed or captured. While Army Group Centre was being crushed, Army Group North was being cleaved in two and forced into retreat towards East Prussia and the Baltic States. This level of attrition puts in perspective the Anglo-American sacrifices on D-Day.

Now when the visitor to Normandy stands on the bluffs at the St. Laurent cemetery and looks down at Easy Red and Green, it is worth pondering the impact that the panzers might have had here on, or shortly after, D-Day. It is also worth recalling the contribution made by Allied deception operations that fixed German reserves in the 15th Army sector towards the Pas de Calais.

Had even a company of German tanks been able to arrive in force on the 6th June or D+1, against the fragile Allied lodgment at Omaha Beach, it is likely that their intervention would have been decisive.

Allied Combined Operations: the Second Front

The intelligence preparations for the Second Front had actually commenced in 1941 as part of a general analysis of occupied Europe. In October of that year, Prime Minister Winston Churchill had summoned Lord Louis Mountbatten back from the Fleet to take command of Combined Operations Headquarters. The direction that he received from the Prime Minister was truly inspiring given that British interests were at their lowest ebb. Churchill issued him with the following order:

'I now want you to start the preparations for our great counter-invasion of Europe. Unless we can land overwhelming forces and beat the Nazis in battle in France, Hitler will never be defeated. So this must be your prime task. I want you to work out the philosophy of invasion, to land and advance against the enemy. You must collect the most brilliant planners in the three services to help you. You must devise and design new landing craft, appurtenances and appliances and train the three services to act together as a single force in combined operation. All other headquarters in England are engaged on defensive measures; your Headquarters must think only

of offence.'

Having taken up the appointment Mountbatten established a philosophy that would assist both him and his successors in designing the campaign plan for the Second Front. He recognized that the Allies must:

Lord Louis Mountbatten

'Firstly be certain of obtaining a firm lodgment at the desired place on the enemy-held coast against all known defences.

Secondly, to break out of the beachheads while reinforcements of men, vehicles, munitions, and stores continued ceaselessly to follow up the spearhead no matter what the weather conditions during the following weeks.

And thirdly, at the same time to keep the main enemy forces as far from the landing area by deception and prevent them, when they discovered the deception, from moving reinforcements to the landing area faster than the build-up of the invasion force, by bombing all road and rail communications over a wide area for several months beforehand.'

In comparison to the gloating German response, Lord Louis Mountbatten's rapidly growing staff at Combined Operations Command drew very different lessons from Operation Jubilee. The British produced a forthright and very constructive Combined Report on the Dieppe Raid that was signed by Mountbatten in October 1942. Lieutenant General Morgan and his staff certainly benefited from the report and its associated lessons learnt. With the advantage of hindsight one can now read the report's 'Lesson of Greatest Importance' and set it against events at Omaha twenty months later. The report stated:

'The Lesson of Greatest Importance is the need for overwhelming fire support, including close support, during the initial stages of the attack. It is not too much to say that, at present, no standard naval vessel or craft has the necessary qualities or equipment to provide close inshore support. Without such support any assault on the enemy-occupied coast of Europe is more and more likely to fail as the enemy's defences are extended and improved.'

The other lessons learned are included in the Appendices. Ultimately, although the cost was terrible, the experience gained at

Dieppe, and then subsequently in North Africa and Sicily would prove essential to Eisenhower's 'Great Crusade.' Mountbatten later assessed that for every casualty suffered at Dieppe the Allies had saved 10 men in Normandy.

In April 1943 Lieutenant General Morgan, Chief of Staff to the as yet un-named Supreme Allied Commander (COSSAC) had warned his team 'the term planning staff has come to have a sinister meaning. It implies the production of nothing but paper. What we must contrive to do somehow is to produce not only paper but action.' The following month in Washington, Roosevelt and Churchill together with their military advisors agreed to launch an offensive against the Atlantic Wall in 1944. Over the next month COSSAC and the Combined Operations Command completed a

highly detailed military appreciation. They concluded at a conference, code named RATTLE, that Normandy was the optimal target for the invasion. Roosevelt and Churchill endorsed this at the Quebec Conference (QUADRANT) in August 1943. A pro-visional date of 1st May 1944 was identified for D-Day under the code named OVERLORD.

One of the foremost deductions in the COSSAC appreciation was that the Allies could not launch the invasion head-on against a fortified port, nor could they count on capturing such a facility during the critical build-up phase. It was inevitable that once the Allies had shown their hand the Germans would be rushing re-

Lieutenant General Morgan (COSSAC), Chief of Staff

inforcements up to the lodgment area to first contain and then destroy the forces in the beachhead. As General Bradley said in his address to the Press on board USS *Augusta* on Saturday evening, 3rd June 1944:

'You've got to remember that just as soon as we land, this business becomes primarily a business of build-up. For you can almost always force an invasion – but you can't always make it stick.'

The outcome of this decisive race to achieve numerical and materiel superiority would depend on the Allies' ability to land, deploy and subsequently supply the combat forces designated for Operation Overlord. A port facility would therefore be critical. German intelligence had as yet no knowledge of the Mulberry concept, so in the absence of an alternative, Hitler's fortress-port policy made considerable sense. By denying the Anglo-American forces any substantial dock facilities, Hitler hoped to starve any second front of the necessary logistic resources required to achieve a decisive build-up and concentration of force for a breakout towards the Reich.

In isolation Hitler may have been right. However, Operation Neptune was the opening stage of a much larger, combined and joint campaign. Once ashore the Allied armies would be sustained by vast stocks of materiel and while they would be struggling to build-up their combat power in the lodgment area, the combined naval fleets and air forces of Britain and the United States would be supporting and protecting them. The Allied air forces would prove to be particularly effective in disrupting German road, rail and air communications, thereby hampering or delaying the arrival of German reinforcements in the battle area. Rommel had recognized that by 1944 the very nature of war had changed and that even the veteran units from the East were in for a shock. Fritz Bayerlain, the commander of Panzer Lehr, recalled Rommel's prophetic words:

'Our friends from the East cannot imagine what they're in for here. It's not a matter of fanatical hordes to be driven forward in masses against our line, with no regard for casualties and little recourse to tactical craft; here we are facing an enemy who applies all his native intelligence to the use of his many technical resources, who spares no expenditure of material and whose every operation goes its course as it had been the subject of repeated rehearsal. Dash and doggedness no longer make a soldier...'

**General Fritz Bayerlain
Commander of Panzer Lehr**

The Allied Joint and Combined Campaign Plans Evolve

After many debates Churchill and Roosevelt agreed that General Dwight D. Eisenhower should be the Supreme Allied Commander for Overlord. Eisenhower was notified on 7th December 1943. Five days later in Germany, Hitler appointed Erwin Rommel to establish a new command for the defence of the Atlantic Wall. At the very time that Rommel was making his presence felt along the northwest European coastline, the Allied command team was being appointed and gathered just across the channel on Christmas Eve 1943.

Shortly after being appointed, Montgomery analyzed the plan proposed by COSSAC. He quickly identified critical flaws in the concept of operations, which had been shaped by General Morgan, based on the resources he had been allocated for this mission. Morgan had been working on the assumption that only three divisions could be used in the first wave. Montgomery rightly considered this to be too small a force deployed over too narrow a frontage. He recommended, and obtained Eisenhower's agreement, that the assault should be expanded to a five-division operation with four divisions in the follow-up wave. He reasoned that this would increase the chances of success by stretching the German response over a wider area, providing greater security to the lodgment and facilitating the capture of key objectives, namely the Port of Cherbourg and the road and rail communications hub at Caen. On 21st January these changes were implemented along with a new target date of 31st May 1944.

The decision was made to expand the scale of Overlord by extending the landing area to include the Cotentin (Utah Beach) and the Orne (Sword Beach). It was also decide to use three airborne divisions to secure the flanks and fix German forces in place during the critical and highly vulnerable amphibious landing phase. This expansion of the assault had severe logistic implications for proposed operations in the Mediterranean. The Americans had been determined to mount Operation Anvil – the invasion of Southern France – as a synchronized operation also on D-Day. They wanted to do this in order to split German attention – and any reserve forces – in two different directions. Unfortunately there were insufficient landing craft in the Allied naval inventory to conduct both operations at once. Nor were there sufficient air and naval combat assets to mount a two front attack on France with any degree

Montgomery analyzed the plan proposed by COSSAC to invade Europe. He quickly identified critical flaws in the concept of operations and sought major changes.

of certainty about the outcome. The decision was made after much inter-Allied debate to re-allocate assets from the Mediterranean to the main effort: Operation Neptune-Overlord in Normandy.

The final assault plan divided the land operation into two sectors. In the West the First US Army, under General Bradley, would land on the beaches code named Utah and Omaha. Two American airborne divisions would be dropped, or landed in gliders on the western flank to dislocate the German response and thereby assist the amphibious forces ashore. In the east, the Second British Army under General Miles Dempsey would land on three beaches, code named Gold, Juno and Sword with an infantry division on each. On the eastern flank the 6th Airborne Division would land by parachute and glider and seize the critical bridges over the River Orne and its canal; the Division would also secure the high ground east of the river as a bridgehead for subsequent operations. It was also hoped that these operations would hamper and generally disrupt German deployments from around Caen against the eastern beaches (Sword and Juno). The plan was that the five beaches would be linked up by midnight on D-Day. By setting his initial objectives deep, Montgomery wanted to encourage dash and elan. The greater the depth achieved, the less likely the invasion would be stalled on the beaches, as had happened at Gallipoli in 1915 and Anzio in 1943.

The final date for mounting the operation and the time for the assault to begin were critical command decisions for Eisenhower. The land component wanted to land in darkness in the hope of gaining tactical surprise – particularly across the exposed beaches. The navy and air component commanders preferred to mount daylight operations in order to ensure more accurate bombardments of enemy targets. The navy was also concerned that in poor sea conditions the already complex task of controlling the vast fleet of assault craft would be all the more hazardous and difficult in darkness.

As a result of Rommel's deployment of defensive obstacles on the Norman foreshore, Ramsey and Eisenhower agreed on 1st May 1944 that the assault would have to take place 3-4 hours before high tide, and about 10 minutes after sunrise. The night before the landing would require good moonlight to support the accurate drop of the airborne divisions and the bombing strikes. All these conditions could only be met on about three days in each lunar month. The final factor would be the weather itself, and this could not be forecast with any real degree of accuracy too far ahead. As a result of all these complex factors the actual date and time for D-Day could not be decided until nearer the window of opportunity in late May-early June. But if the invasion was not launched then, it would have to be delayed for several weeks before the correct conditions recurred.

The Joint Campaign: Allied Air Power

By 1944 the Allies had developed an ever improving joint force capability (the art of operating and exploiting the synergy between separate military services) within a combined (the operations of multinational forces in a coalition or an alliance) environment. On 14th April 1944 the overall direction of Allied strategic forces passed to General Eisenhower. He promptly instructed his British deputy, Air Chief Marshal Sir Arthur Tedder, to act as an intermediary between the various interests of the Allied air commanders in order to create an overall operational plan in support of the forthcoming invasion.

Tedder assisted the Allied effort by shaping, designing and activating a devastating air campaign that would support the expeditionary phase and subsequent land battle in Normandy. With the Allied Expeditionary Air Force under the overall command of Air Chief Marshal Sir Trafford Leigh-Mallory, air forces were assigned to conduct both defensive (force protection) and offensive tasks. To ensure that these were properly integrated within the Neptune phases, Leigh-Mallory considered that:

'..the air operations in immediate and direct support of the land battle should be specially co-ordinated and directed. I, therefore, decided to establish a small operational organisation to be known as Advanced Allied Expeditionary Air Force [AEAF]. Under my general direction, the Commander AEAF was given the task of directing and coordinating the planning for and operations of such forces of the Ninth Air Force and Second Tactical Air Force as were allotted to him from time to time.'

Amidst fierce argument and bitterness Tedder and Leigh-Mallory succeeded in achieving a concentration of effort from the Allied air forces that would make a significant contribution to the overall campaign. The Allied air plan for Neptune-Overlord stated that the general aim of the Allied air forces would be:

'To attain and maintain an air situation which would assure freedom of action for our Forces without effective interference by

enemy air forces and to render air support to our Land and Naval Forces in the achievement of this objective.'

To achieve this aim the following tasks were to be fulfiled in a four-phase air campaign:

The four phase campaign was organized as follows:

Phase 1. The first phase of air operations consisted of air interdiction of enemy naval and air assets in the Channel area, in addition to extensive air reconnaissance operations.

Phase 2. This phase commenced in March 1944 and was known as the preparatory phase. As D-Day approached the combined weight of air operations would fall on targets associated with the invasion. This included the use of heavy bombers to attack fortresses, naval facilities and lines of communication (rail, road and surveillance assets such as coastal radar stations). During this phase two out of three raids were still being conducted away from Normandy to maintain the deception plan.

Phases 3 and 4. These last two phases were designed to support the actual invasion and the subsequent battle for Normandy. The scale of effort was remarkable: 54 fighter squadrons were designated to provide beach cover, while another 15 squadrons protected the fleet. An additional 33 fighter squadrons were tasked for escort duties with the bombers and airborne forces. 36 bomber squadrons were to provide direct support to the land battle with 7 additional squadrons of Spitfires and Mustangs providing fire control. In total some 5,000 fighters were operating over the invasion area in addition to the medium and heavy bombers. Between 6th and 30th June this Allied air fleet would conduct a total of 163,403 air sorties.

Using this vast air capability at the Allies disposal, Tedder directed Bomber Command to attack targets throughout France by night while the U.S. Eighth Air Force along with fleets of Allied fighter bombers attacked other selected targets by day.

The outcome of this air campaign was dramatic. From January 1944 to D-Day the French rail system was strangled as a result of the thorough execution of the Transportation Plan. German controlled French rail traffic had dropped to a mere 30 percent of its 1943 totals. Essential bridges leading to the Normandy battle area were destroyed and all major roads and railways severely damaged. To support the deception plans for D-Day these attacks were not confined to Normandy alone. Raids were conducted across northern France and Belgium. The Seine and Loire River bridges were particularly singled out for methodical destruction in May 1944,

From January 1944 to D-Day the French rail system was strangled as a result of air attacks throughout France by night and by day

thereby impeding the movement of the critical panzer and panzergrenadier divisions into Normandy after D-Day.

Because of the very thorough and integrated Allied planning involved in every aspect of Operation Overlord the Germans were unable to assess this bombing campaign and deduce with any certainty as to where the expected invasion would take place. This confusion was reinforced by the Allied air targeting policy: for every raid inside Normandy two were conducted elsewhere. The effects of the bombing operations were severe and felt throughout the West. In 1946 Lieutenant General Friedrich Dihm, former Special Assistant to Erwin Rommel, stated in an interrogation conducted by the US Army:

> *'Except for this air supremacy, it would have been possible, in my opinion, to prevent a successful invasion during the first days after the initial assault. These were the most critical days for the Allies. Later, the constant and increasing reinforcement of the Allies could be less and less equalized by the arrival of German reinforcements, hindered by the destruction of important traffic routes.'*

It is important to realize that the air plans for Overlord were also closely related to the general strategic air offensive being waged against Germany through 1943-44. The architects of that overall campaign were Lieutenant General Carl Spaatz, Commander US

Strategic Air forces in Europe, and Air Chief Marshal Sir Arthur 'Bomber' Harris, Commander-in-Chief of Britain's Bomber Command. These two very powerful commanders were known as the 'Bomber Barons.' In philosophical terms, they were in direct opposition to Eisenhower's deputy, Tedder, who wanted to use all available means in support of the forthcoming invasion. The 'Bomber Barons' were vehemently opposed to any suggestion that their strategic assets be diverted from their campaign against the heartland of the Reich, to what they considered as tactical operations in support of Overlord. After a lengthy and highly political debate, common sense prevailed and a cohesive air plan emerged in support of Overlord.

The air plan combined the strengths of both the bomber force and tactical air assets with devastating results. Part of Tedder's overall strategy was to draw out the enemy air force and destroy it in combat. The effects of this policy were dramatic. By June 1944 the Allies dominated the skies above the Neptune-Overlord area. From January to June 1944 a total of 2,262 German fighter pilots had been killed out of a force averaging 2,283 at any one time. In May 1944 alone, 25 percent of the total fighter pilot force had died during a relentless Anglo-American campaign to rid the skies over France of enemy aircraft. From April 1944 relentless attacks were mounted against enemy airfields within a 130-mile radius of the invasion beaches.

One additional effect of this campaign was to force the Germans to withdraw and disperse their remaining limited air capability away from the French coast and place these valuable and limited

A Junkers 88 is shot to ribbons in a ground strafing run. By June 1944 the Allies dominated the skies above the Neptune-Overlord area.

assets well to the rear in the Paris area. It is hardly surprising that the Luftwaffe would be notably ineffective on D-Day. Only two German fighters would strafe the beaches during the daytime.

Beyond the lodgment area Allied air power would be a major contributor to the disruption and delay of German troop and equipment movements. One mobile *Kampfgruppe* ordered to move from Brittany took ten days to reach the invasion front as a result of sustained Allied air attacks.

Unfortunately at the tactical level even the might of the Allied air forces fell short of expectations at Omaha Beach on D-Day. At 0600 hours some 480 B-24 Liberator bombers of the US 8th Air Force attacked 13 targets along the coast. In limited visibility many of those raids were initiated late for fear of bombing the convoys or landing craft already heading in to the shore to meet their H-Hour at 0630 hours. As a result, the bombs fell harmlessly up to 3 miles inland leaving the defences intact and the flat open beach un-cratered and thus devoid of cover for the approaching waves of assault troops.

The Joint Campaign: Naval Forces

While Allied air forces could shape the battlefield, provide force protection and isolate the invasion area it would inevitably fall to the combined fleet of the Allied navies to get the expeditionary armies to their objectives. Allied naval forces were under the overall command of Admiral Sir Bertram Ramsay. His tasks included the design and preparation of Operation Neptune the maritime element of the Overlord invasion plan. Some 4,100 ships and craft of all types would be involved in the initial assault, each vessel choreographed into the grand design, the object of which – as Ramsay stated in his orders – was to 'secure a lodgment on the continent from which further offensive operations can be developed'.

Ramsay's responsibilities included the carriage and sustainment of the invasion forces in Normandy. In addition naval gunfire would form a

Admiral Sir Bertram Ramsay

vital, devastating component in the overall fire support provided to the ground forces during their assault and into the follow-on phase when the lodgment would be secured. Naval gunfire would also prove to be a decisive component in offensive and defensive fire missions during the Battle of Normandy. This intimate tactical support would continue while the front line remained within range of the ships' guns sited off the beaches. Naval assets would also play a major role in the Fortitude deception operations by supporting a feint towards the Pas de Calais.

The Western Naval Task Group was responsible for Omaha and Utah Beaches. The Task Group was under the overall command of

Rear Admiral Alan G. Kirk

Rear Admiral Alan G. Kirk in the USS *Augusta*. Lieutenant General Omar Bradley would accompany him on that ship. Kirk was responsible for supporting Bradley's US First Army with over 200 vessels of all types. His command was divided into subordinate Task Forces (TF): TF 125 comprised of Assault Force 'U' aimed at Utah Beach under Rear Admiral Don P. Moon. TF 124 was under command of Rear Admiral John L. Hall USN, destined for Omaha Beach. Hall's mission was to transport and deliver the expeditionary force to Omaha Beach and provide both force protection and offensive naval gunfire support to the ground forces and his subordinate assault craft. Major General Leonard T. Gerow commanding the US V Corps accompanied Hall. These two commanders were co-located for the assault in the command ship USS *Ancon*, a sophisticated headquarters vessel specifically designed to direct amphibious operations. In 1944 the very existence of such a naval platform was classified as a secret.

Part of the navy's force protection tasks included minesweeping the sea crossing and inshore waters. A total of 278 British and American navy minesweepers would perform this vital task by clearing safe routes for the vast convoys of transports and landing craft. Initially, ten cleared corridors were created through the German mine barriers both in the Channel and inshore. These narrow corridors were then expanded into cleared areas so that bombardment ships and the transports could manoeuvre more freely off the beaches.

An additional protective task involved the defence of the invasion fleet from enemy naval action. On D-Day the Allied naval commanders were acutely aware of the threat posed by German 'schnellboots' (motor torpedo boats or E-Boats as they were known by the Allies) stationed in the fortified ports of Le Havre and Cherbourg. Just over five weeks earlier, on 28th April 1944, the American convoy T4 had been attacked by E Boats in Lyme Bay off the Dorset coast, while taking part in Exercise Tiger. This exercise was a dress rehearsal for the US VIIth Corps. The convoy was carrying men from the 4th Infantry Division destined for the operation against Utah Beach on D-Day. The three-mile long convoy consisted of eight LCTs under the escort of HMS *Azalea*. Shortly after 0200 hours the convoy was attacked by nine E-Boats from the 5th and 9th Flotillas in Cherbourg. The results were devastating. Three LCTs were struck in less than 25 minutes. US personnel commented afterwards that the Germans had them 'trapped and hemmed-in like a bunch of wolves circling a wounded dog.' A total of 749 men were killed. One unit, the 3206th Quartermaster Company was annihilated.

At dawn the following day rescue ships approached the area. Aboard HMS *Obedient* Julien Perkin recalled:

> 'We arrived in the area at daybreak and the sight was appalling. There were hundreds of bodies of American servicemen in full battle gear, floating in the sea. Many had their limbs and even their heads blown off... Of all those we took on board there were only nine survivors.'

Fortunately on D-Day the combined fleet would prove highly effective in deterring further German forays from the ports on the

An E-Boat returning to base after having discharged its torpedoes. On 28th April 1944, nine E-Boats from the 5th and 9th Flotillas, based at Cherbourg, attacked American convoy T4 in Lyme Bay off the Dorset coast. The results were devastating, a total of 749 American servicemen lost their lives.

flanks of the invasion area. Only one ship would be lost to German naval action on D-Day and that was the Royal Norwegian Navy's destroyer, the *Svenner*, supporting Force 'S' off Ouistreham. It seems that the *Kriegsmarine* had ignored Admiral Dönitz's speech on 17th April 1944 when he demanded of his units: 'Throw yourselves recklessly into the fight... any man who fails to do so will be destroyed in shame and ignominy'.

The Allied navy also performed a vital fire support function bombarding German positions. The naval 'Gunfire Support Plan List of Targets' for Force O was an astonishingly detailed document. It was dated 20 May 1944, as was the Schedule of Fires that listed the fire support ships, targets, timings and number of rounds. This was a highly sophisticated plan in itself.

The Bombardment Group for Omaha was under command of Rear Admiral C.F. Bryant USN. His Group included two American battleships, the *Arkansas* and *Texas*, four light cruisers (two, the *Montcalm* and *Georges Leygues* were crewed by General Charles DeGaulle's Free Frenchmen), and the destroyers of DESRON 18. The Bombardment Group's mission was to 'assist in ensuring the safe and timely arrival of our forces by the engagement of hostile coastal defences'. They would engage their appointed targets from 0550 hours through to 0630 hours. The main effort was focussed on German coastal gun batteries (Pointe du Hoc receiving special attention from the USS *Texas*) and fortifications on the beaches. Once the land forces commenced their assault at 0630 hours the navy would provide on-call fire support.

To provide accurate targeting the Neptune bombardment forces were supported by 104 spotter planes and 39 Forward Observer Bombardment (FOB). The FOB parties consisted of naval personnel equipped with radio communications back to the ships and trained to operate with the ground forces ashore. The air spotters were equipped with slow moving Piper aircraft, ideal for loitering and observing over the battlefield. The air spotters made a vital contribution to the effectiveness of naval gunfire support during the landing phase. As a result of their target indication and adjustment of fire, targets were actually engaged up to 17 miles inland. In total five bombardment groups were organized to engage the 23 German shore based batteries located in Normandy. In addition, each ship was given one battery as its primary target. Reconnaissance and intelligence gathering operations prior to D-Day had identified these battery positions in great detail.

The naval support at Omaha Beach can be divided into three geographical areas: the Pointe du Hoc, the centre beaches called Dog and Easy where the 116th and 115th Regimental Combat Teams of 29th Division landed, and Easy Red and Fox Beach, where the 1st Divisions 16th, 18th and 15th RCTs would land. The sequence of events in each area followed a well rehearsed pattern: minesweeping, disembarkation from the transport ships into assault craft eleven miles from the coast, preparatory bombardment and the assault conducted by successive waves of both amphibious tanks, and a variety of landing craft carrying troops and vehicles ashore.

Unfortunately the preliminary bombardment at Omaha Beach would prove insufficient to disrupt or destroy the defences to any significant degree. In addition, with the defences sited to fire along the beach in enfilade (fire applied to a target from the flank rather than head on), many bunkers and gun emplacements were hard to see from offshore. It was not until it became clear that things were going awry on the beach as the first wave of assault troops floundered under withering German defensive fires, that the bombardment force closed on the beach to provide intimate support. During this assault phase the agile destroyers and even the larger vessels would be engaging opportunity targets in a desperate effort to help the men pinned-down on the beach. Many of the destroyers would actually come so close to the beach that they would be scraping their keels as they pummelled the German fortified positions. Even the capital ship USS *Arkansas* would risk grounding by closing on the beach to provide accurate and devastating fire from its 14 inch guns as the men of the 1st and 29th Divisions struggled ashore.

During his subsequent and increasingly desperate attempts to contain and eliminate the bridgehead, Rommel reported that,

'our operations in Normandy are tremendously hampered ...by the superiority of the enemy air force [and] the effect of the heavy naval guns.'

After the war other German generals would also praise the naval gunfire support provided in Normandy. Field Marshal Von Rundstedt said, 'the fire from your battleships was a main factor in hampering our counter-attacks. This was a big surprise... '

As the battle for the beachhead developed into the battle for Normandy, the land and air forces (operating from forward air landing grounds just behind the frontline) were very dependent on sea lines of communication to provide the necessary logistic support to the campaign. Admiral Ramsay established a complex structure of naval control headquarters to manage beach control, turn around control of shipping, and a Combined Operations Repair Organization. Add to this the Combined Operations Tug Organization and one can imagine the thorough planning and command and control requirements of this astonishing joint and combined campaign plan.

On top of these tasks the Allied navy would require 10,000 men and 160 tugs just to move the Mulberry harbours into place by D+4 at Omaha and Arromanches. Ramsay also had responsibility for

establishing the initial fuel supply routes into Normandy. Prior to Cherbourg being captured, this was handled in part through Port en Bessin, where flexible steel pipes were used to offload tankers off the coast. By D+18 the Allies were able to draw 600 tons of fuel per hour into France.

The invasion and subsequent campaign were characterized by this kind of innovative and dynamic approach to a large number of complex and challenging requirements. Any one of those challenges, if left un-addressed, could in their own way have placed a brake on the campaign, or worse still affected the speed and outcome of critical military operations.

**Lieutenant General
Omar N. Bradley**

The US Ground Force Component

In October 1943 Lieutenant General Omar N. Bradley took over operational command of all American ground forces in Britain. By January 1944 these numbered over 700,000 men organized in eleven divisions. For D-Day Bradley would command the First US Army. This Army consisted of the V US Corps destined for Omaha Beach, under the command of Major General Gerow, and the VII US Corps under command of Major General 'Lightning Joe' Collins. Each Corps was composed of three infantry divisions, corps troops and many specialist attachments.

V US Corps

Major General Leonard 'Gee' Gerow was an experienced soldier. He had graduated from the Virginia Military Academy in 1911.

During the First World War he served in France with the American Expeditionary Forces Signal Corps Staff. After the War he served in the War Department from 1920 through to 1941. During that time he attended the Army Command and General Staff School at Fort Leavenworth, Kansas. He graduated eleventh out of 245 students. A creditable performance on a course that 'Lightning Joe' Collins had described in his memoirs as 'probably the most important in the entire system of military education, and [was] to prove invaluable in World War II.' Gerow's inter-war service included appointments in the War Plans and Organization Department, the

Major General Leonard 'Gee' Gerow

office of the Assistant Secretary of War, and the War Plans Division where he was appointed to be Chief of Staff. In 1942 he briefly commanded the 29th Division before assuming command of V Corps in July 1943. At that time V Corps was the only American Corps command in Britain and only contained the 29th Infantry Division. It was not until November 1943 that the 1st Division would join the 29th Division in England.

In February 1945 General Eisenhower would review his subordinates in order of priority and value of service to their country. Eisenhower rated Bradley at the top of his list; George Patton was rated fourth and Gerow came eighth. This was a substantial compliment and certainly a testament to Gerow's performance in command of V Corps both in Normandy and up to his hand-over of command in January 1945.

The Assault Divisions

Of the eleven American divisions in Britain only four had any previous combat experience. On D-Day at Omaha Beach, only the 1st Division could claim to have seen extensive action prior to D-Day and their reputation was already quite remarkable. Transferring to Britain in August 1942 from New York, the Division consisted of three Regimental Combat Teams (RCT). On 9th August these Regiments and the divisional troops had taken over Tidworth Barracks in Wiltshire. Then, from 8th November 1942 through to D-Day the 'Big Red One' conducted the invasion at Oran in North

Africa, fought through Algeria, landed at Gela in Sicily and fought throughout that campaign before being shipped to Britain for the forthcoming invasion of Normandy. This breadth of experience may well have been critical to their eventual success at Omaha Beach on 6th June. Bradley certainly felt that the Division had been vital to the outcome of D-Day. He later stated that

'Had a less experienced division than the 1st stumbled into this crack resistance, it might easily have been thrown back into the channel. Unjust though it was, my choice of the 1st to spearhead the invasion probably saved us at Omaha Beach and a catastrophe on the landings.'

Even Eisenhower remarked, after the Battle for Normandy was over that:

'I know your record from the day you landed in Africa, then Sicily. I am beginning to think that the 1st Division is a sort of Praetorian Guard.'

This praise was well founded and echoed by Don Whitehead the Associated Press correspondent who wrote:

'...in all its battles in Africa, Sicily, France, Belgium and Germany, there never was one quite like Omaha Beach. In that battle alone the Fighting First won a niche among the immortals of American history.'

In contrast, the 29th 'Blue and Gray' Division lacked any operational experience in early 1944. In some ways it was a typical example of the vast majority of American infantry units committed to battle in northwest Europe, while in other ways it could claim to be rather unique. Major General Charles H. Gerhardt took command of the Division in July 1943 at the same time that his predecessor, Leonard Gerow, was taking over V Corps. Gerhardt was a 1917 graduate of West Point. He had served in France in 1918 with the American 89th Division. As he assumed command of the 29th in the summer of 1943, the Division was about to start amphibious training at the Assault Training Centre on Woolacombe beach. Each of his Regimental Combat Teams would spend three weeks at the Centre before conducting full-scale assault rehearsals at Slapton Sands at the end of 1943.

By 1944 the Division had acquired a well-established reputation as a highly disciplined, well trained and vigorously lead National Guard formation

under 'Uncle Charlie' Gerhardt. In the spring of 1944 the Division was training with the veteran 1st Division on the south coast of England. On one occasion as the troops chanted their battle-cry, 'Twenty-nine, lets go!' a rather more worldly member of the 1st Division responded with 'Go ahead Twenty-nine, we'll be right behind you!' The veterans of North Africa and Sicily roared with laughter. Yet combined with Gerow's earlier efforts, Gerhardt had created a strong sense of professionalism, divisional identity, and a spirited aggressiveness that would pay off in Normandy and earn the respect of their veteran brothers in 1st Division.

The Division was primarily recruited from Maryland and Virginia where the 29th Division's armouries (equivalent to British Territorial Army drill halls) were located. This meant that the recruits had a strong regional focus and identity. Unfortunately when such units enter combat, the losses incurred tend to have a devastating effect on a small-localized group of families back home. When the 29th Division 's 116th RCT came ashore on D-Day and incurred terrible losses the effects of those casualties would be most felt in Bedford, Lynchburg and Roanoke, in southern Virginia where A, B and D companies were recruited and based. Bedford, is a small town of 3,000 people; it would lose 23 men at Omaha Beach on D-Day. Twenty-two of those men were from Company A 116th RCT, among them were three sets of brothers. Sergeant John Slaughter of Company D later observed:

'Raymond and Bedford Holback was killed. Raymond was wounded and lay on the beach. Then when the tide came in he was washed out to sea and drowned. They never found his body. He was carrying a bible and it washed up upon the sand. The day after D-Day a GI found it. It had Raymond's name and address in Bedford inside and the soldier mailed it to the family. On the Saturday (D-Day was a Tuesday) their family got a telegram that Bedford was killed and then on Sunday they got another one saying Raymond was too. There were two Parkers killed. Then Roy and Ray Stevens who were twins, Roy was wounded and Ray was killed.'

In 1998 John Slaughter was still actively lobbying for a D-Day memorial to be erected in Bedford to pay tribute to the men who lost their lives in France 54 years earlier.

Like so many other Allied infantry formations, Gerhardt's Division would be destined to suffer terrible losses not only on D-Day but also subsequently during the campaign to liberate occupied Europe and conquer Germany through 1944-45. As it was, the 29th would quickly make up for its lack of action prior to assaulting Omaha Beach. It would participate in all 337 days of the northwest European campaign. It would suffer a total of 20,111 battle casualties including 3,720 dead – more than any other American division in World War II except one. These casualty figures should be set against the divisional official establishment of 14,000 personnel. In effect, any soldier in an infantry company who survived D-Day was unlikely to see the war through to its final conclusion physically unscathed. That was the reality of front line operations in this struggle to rid the world of the Third Reich.

The Decisive Task of Force Protection: The Allied Deception Plan

The Allies appreciated that all aspects of operational security (deception, secrecy of intentions, concealment of the force and its movement) would be critical to achieving victory. As COSSAC had soberly warned:

'If the enemy obtains as much as forty-eight hours' warning of the location of the assault area, the chances of success are small, and any longer warning spells certain defeat.'

The security requirements for D-Day were complex, thorough and highly effective. Protective intelligence operations were further enhanced by a very complex, active and well-resourced deception campaign that left the German high command confused as to Allied intentions well into late July 1944. Deception operations were essential to the outcome of the invasion. In February 1944 OB West had 53 divisions under command. By the 3rd June 1944 this had increased to 60 divisions (50 infantry and 10 panzer or panzergrenadier divisions). Of those divisions now in the West, 36 (30 infantry and 6 panzer or panzergenadier divisions) were in Rommel's Army Group B located along the coast from Holland to the Bay of Biscay. In order to prevent the Germans from winning the race to build-up forces in Normandy during the crucial days after 6th June an effective deception plan was vital.

Plan Bodyguard was the overall cover operation for the Normandy invasion. It was 'a vast, complex web of trickery spun right across Europe, from North Cape to Cairo and from Moscow to Algiers.' The plan included a multiplicity of threats designed to divide the enemy's attention and fix Hitler's forces in areas far removed from Normandy. Bodyguard consisted of the following component plans:

Fortitude North: threatened invasion of Norway
Fortitude South: threat to the Pas de Calais
Zeppelin: threat to the Balkans
Vendetta and **Ferdinand**: threats to the western Mediterranean
Ironside: threat to the French coast on the Bay of Biscay.
Each of these plans was further reinforced by diplomatic initiatives such as Royal Flush. This was directed at the Scandinavian governments; and Copperhead that featured the visit to Gibraltar of General Montgomery's 'double.' Other ancillary, tactical deceptions were established and conducted on the evening of 5-6th June to protect the actual D-Day landings. These included:

Dropping dummy parachutists to mislead and draw out local German reserves, two of these can be viewed in the Museum of Peace in Caen or in the airborne museum at St Mere Eglise,

Initiating and directing sabotage operations by the French Resistance, particularly against transportation and communications systems,

Deploying Special Forces in depth to hamper the deployment of operational reserves,

Jamming and decoying the remaining German coastal radars with chaff or decoy operations by air and sea assets,

Conducting a well-resourced and effective feint at the Pas de Calais.

Part of the Allied deception plan - the appearance of 'Monty' in the Mediterranean. This was in fact Clifton James - Monty's double.

The crucial deception operation in all this was Fortitude South, the fictitious but credible threat to the Pas de Calais. The most effective military deceptions are those that reinforce an enemy's preconceptions. The Pas de Calais made complete sense to the Germans as the target for the impending invasion: it was the shortest route across the Channel and offered the best approach to the Reich, a mere 150 miles from these beaches. This short approach to the heart of the Reich also offered the Allies the greatest opportunity to use their fighter aircraft to best effect. The short distance and flight time from the British southeast coast would allow even the shorter-range fighters to loiter over the battlefield for a greater length of time.

To reinforce the credibility of this deception, Fortitude South portrayed the presence of a massive force in southeast England, the

notional First United States Army Group (FUSAG), commanded by General George Patton. The Germans took the bait enthusiastically. This was in Charles Cruikshank's words,

A dummy Sherman tank is moved into position – one of many placed in the South East of England to help convince the Germans that landings would take place in the Pas de Calais.

'... the largest, most elaborate, most carefully-planned, most vital, and most successful of all the Allied deception operations. It made full use of the years of experience gained in every branch of the deception art – visual deception and misdirection, the deployment of dummy landing craft, aircraft, and paratroops, fake lighting schemes, radio deception, sonic devices, and ultimately a whole fictitious army group.'

Proof of the German obsession with the Pas de Calais comes from a report dated 10th July 1944 – more than a month after D-Day – from Rommel's headquarters to Von Rundstedt in OB West. The report stated,

'The enemy has at present thirty five divisions in the landing area. In Great Britain anther sixty are standing-to, fifty of which may at any moment be transferred to the continent... We shall have to reckon with large scale landings of 1st US Army Group in the North for strategic co-operation with the Montgomery Army Group in a thrust on Paris.'

Those sixty divisions never existed. Ultimately, the deception caused sufficient doubt and hesitation that the Germans held eighteen divisions totally uncommitted in their 15th Army near Calais during the critical week following 6th June. By sustaining the ruse into July (Fortitude South II), the Allies successfully tied-down more forces north of the Seine after the invasion of Normandy than had been there prior to 6th June. Astonishingly, major withdrawals from northeastern France and Belgium were not initiated until after the Allied breakthrough (Operation Cobra) at Avranches finally demonstrated that the Battle of Normandy had been lost.

CHAPTER TWO

OVERLORD ASSAULT PLAN:
OMAHA BEACH AND POINTE DU HOC

General Military Assessment of the Lodgment Area

Under the auspices of COSSAC's initial study of invasion options, the European coastline from Norway to the Pyrenees had been analyzed and studied in detail. This remarkable effort came to fruition in late 1943. The planning staff had narrowed the choice to two specific areas, the Pas de Calais and Normandy from the Cotentin peninsula to Caen. The Pas de Calais had much to commend it. The sea and air crossings would be very short and once ashore the assault force would be within striking distance of the industrial heartland of Germany, the Ruhr. Furthermore, the vital air cover, so essential to expeditionary operations would be easy to provide. It seemed the most obvious course of action; a point not lost on the Germans who had conducted a similar analysis and massed formidable defences, supported by mobile and static forces, in the area.

On the other hand the Normandy coast was less strongly held and the beaches, being partially sheltered from prevailing westerly winds by the Cherbourg Peninsula, were therefore more suitable for landing the large quantities of vehicles and stores needed. The six-fathom line also ran near enough to the shore in Normandy to allow larger transports to unload near the beach and bombardment ships to close with and engage coastal defences. The key port at Cherbourg, in the Cotentin, was also ideally suited for the entry to France of British and American seaborne reinforcements and bulk logistics – assuming that its facilities could be captured quickly and intact. The counter arguments against Normandy included the length of the crossing from Britain. Being 70 miles further, Allied aircraft would have less time over the objective than they would over Calais. Nevertheless the joint planning staff was prepared to sacrifice this in favour of other advantages, not the least being the opportunity for tactical surprise.

In August 1943 the Allied leaders met in Quebec and selected Normandy as the battlefield for the so called 'Second Front.' Once this decision had been made to assault Fortress Europe through

Normandy, a more detailed analysis was conducted – within the bounds of security – by the single service staffs and higher tactical headquarters.

Terrain Analysis

A soldier has a unique and very intimate relationship with the ground upon which he lives and fights. It can provide space to manoeuvre, a home below its surface, concealment from view and more importantly, protective cover from fire.

Opposed expeditionary operations such as Gallipoli, Dieppe, Sicily, and Normandy remind even the casual observer that beaches frequently lack any effective protective shelter for an attacking force. From the water's edge to the back-beach area, an assaulting force is usually exposed to the threat of direct and indirect fire and physical engagement in close quarter combat by any moderately competent or robust defence. Omaha is just such an exposed beach. The 7,000 yards of sand and shingle are completely dominated by the 100-foot escarpment above. So why did the Neptune-Overlord planners select this unlikely place, with its natural, very easily defended palisade, to be a crucial assault beach, particularly after the Anglo-Canadian bloodletting at the defended port of Dieppe? The reasons can be found in the overall concept of operations and in an analysis of the Normandy coastline, the offshore currents and tide, and the available routes inland.

An intimate knowledge of the English Channel, and the Baie de la Seine was essential if the Overlord planners were to make an effective choice as to where to land the assault divisions. To that end, intelligence staffs sought information from all available sources on such matters as water depths, beach contours, gradients, tidal patterns, and coastal obstructions such as reefs, soft sand patches, or sandbars. Beyond the beaches the terrain was further assessed for its suitability as a defensible lodgment, as a logistic base for subsequent operations, for the siting of improvised air landing grounds, and for avenues of approach inland for the breakout.

This detailed analysis drew on all sources of information including pre-war holiday postcards and family snapshots gathered from a willing public throughout Britain. Special Forces personnel, in addition to air, navy and army intelligence assets also conducted active military reconnaissance operations. The 'secret army' of local French Resistance operatives also provided timely information. On

Supreme Allied Commander Dwight D. Eisenhower discusses aspects of the invasion with three of his British commanders, Air Chief Marshal Sir Trafford Leigh-Mallory, Air Chief Marshal Sir Arthur W. Tedder (Deputy Supreme Commander), General Sir Bernard Law Montgomery.

display in the Museum of Peace in Caen are examples of their intricate hand-drawn sketches and maps made by these French patriots in Normandy throughout 1943-44. The precision and detail of such intricate work is breathtaking. From bases in England, electronic surveillance systems also monitored all the intercepted radio emissions (Ultra being the most notable) from occupied Europe. Radar sites, command headquarters, and unit locations were detected, identified and integrated into the vast intelligence mosaic that would ultimately shape the Allies' plans for the great counter-invasion in the West.

Morgan 's staff identified that in general, the coastline of western Calvados was interspersed with cliffs exceeding 100 feet in places. Beyond the beaches several low-lying areas were obstructed by marshes. By 1944 German military engineers were conducting deliberate flooding operations to further enhance these low-lying areas as military obstacles. This was particularly evident behind Utah Beach where the causeways from the beach inland to higher ground had been isolated by extensive inundations. The Germans had also conducted similar flooding in the 29th Division 's objective area between Isigny-sur-Mer and Treviers. Here, the River Aure and its flood plain had been transformed into an obstacle to any cross-country vehicle movement.

The COSSAC analysis of Normandy had identified Omaha Beach as a necessary objective. It was, however, recognized as being sub-optimal because of its terrain. The harsh reality was that Normandy offered only a few areas that were suitable for large-scale landing operations. With the expansion of the Neptune assault area to include Sword and Utah Beaches, after Christmas 1943, it was all the more essential that Omaha be taken in order to establish an inter-connected, cohesive front from the Cotentin to the Orne.

The V US Corps Objective: Terrain at Omaha Beach

Offshore, rocky ledges and outcrops reinforced the coast's natural defences. These characteristic barriers to an amphibious assault gave way below the bluffs at Omaha Beach. Here, near the villages of Colleville-sur-Mer and Vierville-sur-Mer, the cliffs and rocks fell away to form a 7,000 yard crescent-shaped strand of beach halfway between Utah and Gold Sectors. If the Allied lodgment was to be effectively established, then Omaha had to be assaulted and a beachhead secured. This would only happen after it had been linked-up with the adjacent British beach to the east (Gold) and the other American beach to the northwest (Utah).

The waters off Omaha Beach add to its evident physical challenges. Here the Baie de la Seine is exposed to northerly and easterly winds. Moderately strong offshore currents are further complicated by eddies and rip tides that have contributed to a series of sandbars and runnels being formed parallel to the beach. These are exposed at low tide, but they created complex conditions for assault craft and wading vehicles on 6th June.

A 300-yard beach is exposed at low tide. This consists of a gently sloping (1:188) gradient of well-compacted sand. After crossing this open, flat section of beach the gradient sharply rises to 1:47 for the last 250 yards below the high water mark. The final beach sector has a gradient of 1:8 before the tidal flat ends at a wave torn embankment beyond which lie a band of large shingle stones and a sea wall. Beyond this wall lies a level, marshy shelf that links the exposed beach to the base of the escarpment, or bluffs.

To this day, the bluffs remain an obstacle to free movement. In 1944 five wooded ravines, or 'draws' as the Americans called them, existed sufficiently wide enough for a narrow road, track, or path to carry traffic up the escarpment to the lateral coast road. No other exits were available for traffic, the slope of the bluffs being too steep for tracked vehicles. The slope even promised to be a stiff climb for an overloaded, wet, and exhausted soldier carrying his equipment.

Inevitably, the draws became the focal points of the German defences and the focus of effort for the assault troops on D-Day. In effect, the military logic of the ground itself would commit the men of the assault divisions to a frontal assault on the enemy's strongest fortifications at Omaha. The beach simply had to be taken, regardless of the cost to the early waves of assault troops.

Settlements and Roads

Today, the settlements in Calvados are still characterized by a Norman adaptation of the Romanesque style. Many buildings are constructed of locally quarried creamy-coloured stone. The older buildings often have cellars that could serve as shelters or fortified strongpoints. A lattice of small roads and tracks connected settlements. In 1944 the Germans frequently made a 5 to 15 mile zone from the seashore inland off-limits though fishermen and farmers were usually allowed to maintain their trades.

The Overlord lodgment area was not suitable for heavy military traffic. At Omaha Beach, the four draws led to the small villages of Vierville-sur-Mer, St-Laurent-sur-Mer, and Colleville-sur-Mer. Routes to and from the beach had been built to support local traffic and threaded through many defiles, or choke points, and across innumerable small, easily obstructed bridges. The only paved road from the beach existed in the Vierville draw. Once inland, the best routes out of the Overlord lodgment area actually emanated from the British left flank via Caen and then to the east and southeast. The V US Corps would be committed to moving inland into the traditional Norman countryside known as bocage which proved to be ideal for defensive warfare.

The Weather and Climate

The climate in the French Department of Calvados is generally mild. However, immediately to the west, the Department of the Manche is the rainiest in all of northern France. In Normandy, maximum precipitation occurs in October, with a secondary peak in June or July. Persistent rains affect off-road vehicle mobility on poorly drained soils, particularly in the Aure valley and behind Utah Beach, where the water tables are close to the surface.

Low clouds and fog often impede visibility in winter and even during the summer when cloud ceilings can be as low as 2,000 feet. May, June and July offer the best chances of good flying weather with up to 5 consecutive clear days often occurring. The summer months are also characterized by very long days and short nights: in 1944 this offered the Allies the best opportunity for air operations while also restricting German troop movement to the shortest possible period of time under the cover of darkness.

The ability to forecast the weather with some degree of accuracy during the May-June window of opportunity for D-Day was vital to both sides. The accuracy of German forecasting had deteriorated throughout 1943-44 as increased Allied air and naval operations had restricted both surface and U-boat operations in the North Sea and the Atlantic. Incomplete meteorological data in late May and early June would lead to Rommel and Von Rundstedt discounting the period 5-6th June as suitable for an invasion. The next opportunity would be in mid-June or as late as August. Based on that assessment many German officers including Rommel went on leave on 5th June 1944. The Allies on the other hand were able to be more precise in their assessment and forecasting.

The Chief Meteorologist to SHAEF was Group Captain John Stagg RAF. His task was to co-ordinate 'the meteorological arrangements for disseminating weather information and advice to the naval, army and air forces, US and British, under the supreme Allied Commander's control.' Stagg was responsible for analyzing all available predictions – including weather data intercepted from German naval ULTRA messages – in order to form an overall weather picture and then brief it to Eisenhower and his senior commanders in the critical days leading up to Eisenhower's momentous decision to invade Europe. On the basis of Stagg's forecasts the decision to 'go' or 'not go' would be made.

In the absence of precise guidance on what were the desired conditions for Neptune-Overlord, Stagg worked on the basis of 'What are the least favourable conditions in which your forces can operate successfully?' To that end, he identified the meteorological conditions for the whole invasion taking into account the various different requirements for naval, amphibious, air, parachute, and ground operations once ashore. The following preconditions are taken from Stagg's notes on the report to SHAEF, on 22nd June 1944:

Meteorological requirements for the Assault

Navy. Surface winds – not exceeding Force 3 (8-12 mph) on shore, Force 4 (13-18 mph) off shore during D-Day to D+2. (Force 5 bearable in open sea but for limited periods only).
No prolonged periods of high winds in the Atlantic causing substantial swell in the Channel.
Visibility – not less than 3 miles.

Air Force. Air Transport
Cloud ceiling at least 2,500 ft and over target. Visibility 3 miles at least.

Heavy Bombers
Not more than 5/10ths cloud below 5,000 ft, cloud ceiling not below 11,000 ft over target.

Medium and Light bombers
Cloud ceiling not less than 4,500 ft over target, visibility at least 3 miles.

Fighter and Fighter bombers
Cloud base not less than 1,000 ft.

Bases. Cloud not below 1,000 ft.

Army. Airborne Landings
Surface wind over the target area not to exceed 20 mph and not gusty. Half moonlight at least.

Ground Forces
Ground dry enough to take heavy vehicles off the main roads

Procedure. January 1944: Directors of Meteorological Services for Air Ministry: Royal Navy, United States Forces, and Chief Meteorological Officer at SHAEF began joint consultations. They devised a routine procedure each week for issuing a forecast for a period of five days. I.e. for five days ahead.

First conference February 1944 (from mid-April conferences every day). They found after the first conferences that it was extremely difficult to predict more than 2 or 3 days ahead. During May (when the weather was mainly settled) the experts forecast 18 days on which the weather was suitable for invasion.

Group Captain J. M. Stagg

It was during the final conferences from 28th May to 5th June 1944 that Stagg was to have such a significant impact on the timing of General Eisenhower's decision to launch this vast operation. After a period of settled weather at the end of May the forecast for 5th June (provisionally selected as D-Day) had deteriorated to such an extent that Eisenhower postponed the invasion by 24 hours. At the 2145 hours conference on Sunday 4th June Stagg could announce a period of 'relatively good weather' on 6th June. Eisenhower then said, after some debate with Ramsey, Montgomery, Tedder, Leigh-Mallory, and Smith:

'Well, I am quite positive we must give the order; the only question is whether we should meet again in the morning.

Well I don't like it but there it is.

Well boys, there it is, I don't see how we can possibly do anything else.'

Thanks to efforts of the meteorological staff a short window of opportunity had been identified, enabling the Supreme Allied Commander to launch D-Day on 6th June.

Intelligence Preparation of the Battlefield
An Overview of German Forces in the Omaha Sector

Any expeditionary operation is by its nature a highly complex mission. It requires intricate planning if the landing force is to be put ashore and supported successfully in the face of hostile defences. The V Corps planning for the assault on Omaha Beach was no exception. The preparation of the 'enemy picture' for this phase of Operation Neptune was remarkable, drawing on all available sources of military intelligence. However, even with this most thorough effort the picture could not be complete.

The men of the 29th and 1st Divisions were to face units from two divisions of the Heer, the 352nd Infantry Division and the 716th Coastal Defence Division. Both these formations were part of the LXXXIV (84th) Corps, commanded by the veteran General Erich Marcks. The 716th Division had been stationed on the Normandy coast since March 1942 holding the sector between the Rivers Vire and Orne. The Division was under command of Major General Richter whose headquarters was sited in quarry tunnels to the north west of Caen at Folie-Couvrechef (now the Caen Memorial Museum). From January to April 1944 his defensive frontage was adjusted or reinforced as additional units from the 77th and 243rd Divisions were integrated into the coastal defences. In May a major adjustment took place when Marcks moved the 352nd Division into the line to the West of the 716th Division's two forward regiments (the I/726th and III/726th). This move went undetected by the Allies until just before D-Day.

On 6th June the V Corps would face:

III/726th deployed between Grandcamp and St. Laurent-sur-Mer, with its battalion headquarters in Jucoville, 3 kms south of Grandcamp-Maisey. The infantry companies were deployed from East to West with the 12th, 5th, 10th, and 11th supported by a further two battalions from the 352nd Infantry Division.

Major General Richter

I/726th deployed between Colleville and Arromanches with its headquarters at Maisons, 5 kms north-west of Bayeux. The 1st, 2nd, 3rd, and 4th companies were sited in the resistance nests in the Omaha sector supported by the 916th Regiment of the 352nd Division.

Two batteries of the 1716th Artillery Regiment stationed south of Maisy and Grandcamp. The batteries were under command of the 352nd Division and equipped with captured French 155-mm and Czech 100-mm artillery guns.

German troops manning a 105mm gun on the Channel coast.

352nd Infantry Division with the 916th Infantry Regiment located at Omaha Beach.

The Divisional commander, General Kraiss, had his headquarters at Molay-Littrey, 14 kms West of Bayeux along the D5, and 21 kms from Omaha Beach. Unlike the 716th Division, Kraiss commanded a well-equipped formation with a strong cadre of Eastern Front veterans. His artillery regiment, commanded by Colonel Ocker, was equipped with new 105-mm and 150-mm guns. While the divisional anti-tank company (352nd Sturmgeschutze-Abteilung) was well equipped with 10 Sturmgeschutze and 14 Marders. This mobile force was deployed in reserve at Bricqueville and Chateau Colombieres behind the Aure marshlands, about 15 Kms south of Pointe du Hoc.

Major Werner Pluskat commanded the I/352 battalion of the divisional artillery regiment. His headquarters was located in Etreham Manor, southeast of Port en Bessin. He had twelve 105-mm guns deployed as follows:

Four guns at Houtteville (I/352nd)
Four guns near Montigny (II/352nd)
Four guns between Formigny and St Laurent.

The IV/352nd could also cover the Omaha Beach area. With its headquarters at Château Agneaux, its twelve 150-mm guns were

deployed around Cambe and at Longueville. This meant that twenty-four guns could fire in support of the forward defences and engage the well planned killing areas on Omaha Beach.

The Organization of German Defences in the Omaha Sector

In May 1944 a signal from the Japanese naval attaché in Berlin to Tokyo was intercepted by British intelligence and decoded. It confirmed that Rommel intended to destroy any invasion 'near the coast, most of all on the beaches'. To that end Rommel had designed an overall defensive scheme for the Normandy

Prior to the invasion Rommel conducted intensive inspections of the German defences.

sector consisting of three belts. The first belt was sited on or immediately behind the beaches and consisted of a narrow band of obstacles covered by fire from coastal defence units. A second line consisting of strongpoints up to five miles inland was under construction. By June 1944 this second line was still incomplete. Unlike Sword Beach further to the East, where 'Hillman' (located behind La Breche D'Hemanville) dominated the back-beach area, there were no such fortresses behind Omaha Beach. So while a vigorous battle could be fought at the water's edge, should any penetration be made up to the crest of the bluffs, the thin belt of initially strong positions along the coast and in the deep draws would became inherently vulnerable to being rolled-up from the flank. This threat could only be countered by local mobile reserves able to mount immediate and effective counter-attacks. Should these initial lines of resistance be penetrated then Rommel would have to call upon his third line of defence, the operational reserves, which could initially fix and then destroy any Allied breakthrough.

To reinforce the foreshore defences, the Germans were seen to be building new obstacles along the Norman coast by February 1944, under the direction of Rommel. The 3rd British Infantry Division's 'Briefing Intelligence Summary' described the defences they would be facing at Sword Beach, however, the general assessment was applicable to all the beaches. It stated:

'Defence activity has quickened since Feb on the occupied coasts, following a tour of inspection in Jan by ROMMEL, who is anti-invasion Army Group Commander. The principal new features are under-water obstacles, the provision of overhead cover for field and medium artillery, an intensification of minelaying, and a tendency to dig field defences on commanding ground 2,000-4,000 yards inland.'

This effort seems to have started at Omaha Beach as late as early April 1944 and was still in progress by D-Day. The obstacles were sited in three bands and designed to impede or defeat landing operations between the high and low water marks across the tidal flat. The outer obstacle strip consisted of reinforced iron structures known as 'Element C.' These gate-like structures stood 10 feet high and had Teller anti-tank mines lashed to their upright supports. The Element C obstacles were sited about 250 yards below the high-water line. The second line of obstacles were sited a further 25 yards toward the beach. This belt consisted of mine or shell tipped wooden posts one foot thick, driven into the sand at a shallow angle and supported by an 'A' frame. These ramp type obstacles were

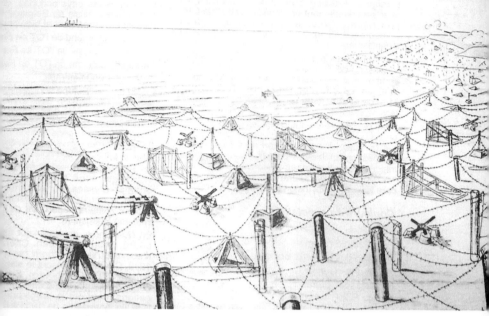

German propaganda drawing illustrating the variety of obstacles being placed on the invasion beaches at Rommel's instigation.

usually sited in two rows between 30-60 feet apart with about 50 feet between individual obstacles. The angle was such that these obstacles would present a major threat to the hull of any approaching vessel as the tide covered the line of 8-10 foot high posts between one and two hours before high tide. On D-Day this particular line of obstacles would prove to be a formidable barrier to landing craft.

The final line of submerged barriers were sited one hundred and thirty yards from the shore. These consisted of steel 'hedgehogs' constructed from three or more angled steel rails crossed at their centres. Each hedgehog stood approximately 5 feet 7 inches high and were sited in rows about 100-110 yards long, each row containing 14-17 hedgehogs at 20 foot intervals. Rows were overlapped and ran continuously across the beachfront and were submerged about an hour before high water. Intelligence assessments stated that these obstacles could sink in the sand. These hedgehogs were sufficiently strong that they could penetrate the hulls of landing craft. It is important to realize that these belts of obstacles were not continuous but were staggered to hamper the direct approach of craft to the beach. On 6th May General Eisenhower described these beach obstacles as 'one of the worst problems of these days.' Two days later, a full assessment had been made of up to date photo-reconnaissance pictures. These high-resolution pictures had allowed the positions of each obstacle to be plotted in detail. As a result of this intelligence, the Allies confirmed that the landings would commence at half-flood on the day that this came at forty minutes after nautical twilight (June 5th was ideal with possible postponements acceptable to the 6th or 7th June).

At Omaha Beach the Germans had not placed loose mines on the tidal flats but sited them above and beyond the shingle embankment towards the bluffs. A barbed wire triple concertina obstacle belt had also been integrated into the landward defences immediately above the shingle. At the western end of the beach the sea wall had been reinforced as a barrier to movement with the addition of further wire obstacles. The marsh and open flat area at the base of the bluffs were also mined and in places, improvised booby traps were set up. These consisted of explosive charges initiated by tripwires sited across the open grassy slopes, or integrated into the barbed wire entanglements. When fired these

A construction team, placing obstacles on the beaches, scatters as an Allied aircraft makes a reconnaissance run.

charges scattered stone and rock, rather like lethal confetti, into the target area. In addition, the Germans had made full use of all available weapons including captured French and British mines from 1940. They also built a small number of marked and fenced dummy minefields with pieces of metal plate buried to deceive mine detectors and prolong any clearance of the area by combat engineers.

These various simple but ingenious obstacles were covered by the fire of weapons sited in defensive positions manned by the coastal defence troops on top of the bluffs. Many of these fire positions were sited in defilade and so protected from the direct fire from ships out to sea. Both plunging and grazing fire could be brought down onto the beach area from all types of weapons. The crescent shape of Omaha Beach also provided the Germans with every advantage to pour flanking fire into the sides of any attacking force.

Beyond the immediate beach area there were a series of fortified strong-points or resistance nests (*Widerstandsnest* or WN) that acted as 'surfaces' against which assaults would be battered. These strongpoints were sited to cover the beach exits or draws. On 6th June several concrete emplacements were still incomplete at Omaha Beach, most notably in the E-1 draw. However, even the partially completed positions were still inherently capable of protecting their crews who could then inflict heavy casualties and delays on the V Corps troops caught in the open, on the flat, open beach. A completed resistance nest normally consisted of approximately a platoon of 30 men equipped with ten machine guns, an artillery piece inside a reinforced bunker and a supporting 50-mm cannon.

The Germans also had over sixty light artillery guns covering Omaha Beach. Eight reinforced concrete bunkers contained 75-mm or 88-mm guns (two at Omaha). A further thirty-five smaller pill-boxes held smaller artillery pieces and an additional eighteen antitank guns ranging from 37-mm to 75-mm were covering likely vehicle approaches. Many of the 50mm and 75mm guns were actually Czech or French guns seized back in 1938 and 1940. These various positions were further reinforced by six tank turrets (from captured vehicles) complete with armament. At WN 60, almost on the boundary between Fox Green and Red, automatic flame-throwers were also in place. The infantry units garrisoning the intervening trenches along the bluffs, were issued with a full range of infantry weapons with a high concentration of machine guns.

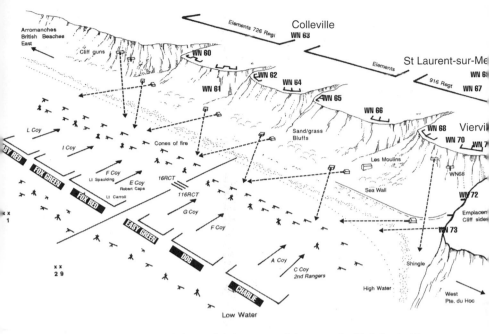

Five exits from the beach formed the strongpoints around which the battle was fought.

There were at least 85 machine guns sited along Omaha Beach.

Indirect fire support could be provided to the forward troops by mortars located in, or to the rear of the fortified strongpoints and by forty rocket pits sited inland on higher ground. Mortars were usually sited in 'Tobrouks,' or open topped reinforced concrete weapons pits. Each of the rocket pits held up to four 32-cm high explosive rockets. WN 67 had some 32-cm rocket launchers integrated into its defences at the top of the D-3 draw. The 32-cm positions were not actually detected and identified until units overran the area from V Corps as they were pushing inland to their initial objectives.

Gun batteries in depth could also provide conventional artillery support. Forward artillery observers were sited in WN 60, 62, 71, 73, and 74. From these strongpoints they were able to adjust indirect artillery fire onto the shore. Lieutenant Frerking for example, was controlling his artillery battery from WN 62 north of Colleville and above the E-3 draw. His dominant position was perfect and allowed him to call and adjust fires with great accuracy. Unfortunately for him, his effectiveness would be constrained by a flawed logistics plan that had placed reserves of battery ammunition too far to the rear, where resupply of the guns depended upon motor transport to bring up the shells. On 6th June even individual German vehicles were viable targets for both observed naval gunfire (controlled by spotter aircraft) and fighters searching for targets of opportunity. As a result of this error of judgement, Frerking's ability to call for indirect artillery fire would be severely restricted by logistic constraints at the very moment when the outcome of the battle hung in the balance.

The Omaha sector was evidently well defended, with a strong integrated defence consisting of mutually supporting and inter-dependent German positions. It is now clear that the Germans had been prevented from extending their beach obstacles down to the low water mark by a shortage of time, manpower, and resources. Other defensive preparations were detected by Allied signal intelligence such as an accelerated deep-water mine laying programme conducted by German navy units. These operations were detected and then analyzed in sufficient detail to assist the Allied minesweepers to clear or mark the obstacle belts in the Channel prior to D-Day. Ashore and inland the Germans also flooded low-lying valleys and fields to limit cross country movement by their more mechanized enemy. They also placed anti-glider landing obstacles in fields considered suitable for landing

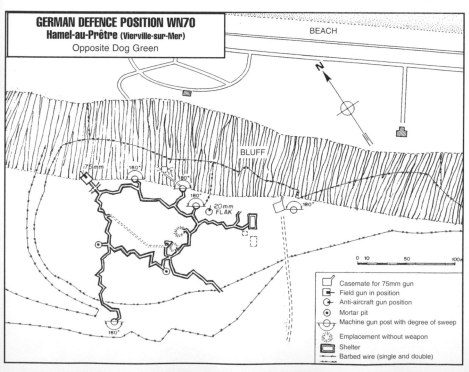

GERMAN DEFENCE POSITION WN70
Hamel-au-Prêtre (Vierville-sur-Mer)
Opposite Dog Green

BEACH

N

BLUFF

75mm

180°

180°

180°

20mm FLAK

180°

180°

0   10   50   100

180°

Casemate for 75mm gun
Field gun in position
Anti-aircraft gun position
Mortar pit
Machine gun post with degree of sweep
Emplacement without weapon
Shelter
Barbed wire (single and double)

grounds. These obstacles consisted of tree trunks embedded in the ground to destroy or impede the flimsy Allied gliders from making a safe landing. Some of these posts – known collectively as 'Rommel's asparagus' – were further enhanced as obstacles to gliders by the attachment of interconnecting wires or cables.

For all their localized, tactical strength the German coastal defences lacked any real depth and Rommel would be severely restricted in his use of the operational and strategic reserves so essential to his defensive concept of operations.

A Failure in Intelligence?

Only one regiment (the 726th Regiment) from 716th Limited Employment (LE) Coastal Defence Division was believed to be defending Omaha sector. The 716th was assessed as being a low quality, over-extended formation with poor morale and about 50% of Poles and Slavs in its ranks. It was also under strength with only 7,771 men, or 35% of the establishment strength of an infantry division.

The 21st Army Group believed that this poor quality division had a frontage of 53 miles from the Vire estuary to the Orne-Dives area in the East. As is now known this was not the whole story. Unfortunately for V Corps, a major adjustment of troops had actually occurred in mid-March 1944. Rommel authorized Generaloberst Dollman (commander of the German 7th Army) to move the 352nd Infantry Division from its reserve location in St Lô to the coastline. Two of its regiments joined the 716th Infantry behind Gold and Omaha Beaches. The division's third regiment moved to Bayeux as a reserve, where it would be located on D-Day.

From April onwards, Allied intelligence had identified the additional reinforcement of forward positions in several coastal sectors. On 14th May 1944 it became clear that this had occurred in the 716th Infantry's area of responsibility. Photo-reconnaissance had confirmed this particularly in the area between Isigny and the River Dives but no indication of the move forward by 352nd had been detected. Montgomery's 21st Army Group staff considered this to be:

> 'A most unsatisfactory state of affairs that we cannot specifically identify all elements which go to make up the sector... This much is evident – that we will on D-Day make contact immediately with 716th 709th, 243rd, the fringe of 711th and, within a very short time,

352nd Infantry and 21st Panzer.'

As late as 4th June the 21st Army Group provided a very accurate assessment of German adjustments. But by this stage the assault divisions were already in their ships and craft awaiting orders to sail for France. The assessment stated:

'For some time now in other areas coastal divisions have been narrowing their sectors, while divisions the role of which has hitherto been read as lay-back have nosed forward into the gaps provided by the reduced responsibility of the coastal divisions... The evidence that the same has happened on the left in the case of 716th Division is slender indeed... yet it should not be surprising if we discovered that it has two regiments in the line and one in reserve, while on its left 352nd has one regiment up and two to play...'

In its 'Intelligence Summary' the 3rd British Infantry Division, destined for Sword Beach, placed the 352nd Division in a dispersed area covering 35-40 miles and with its closest units about 15 miles from Caen it was considered to be:

'Formed from remnants of a division destroyed in Russia. Personnel believed very young or 35-40. Partly mechanized... . Suitably disposed to send troops (? A regt) to strengthen POLAND [codename for Caen] attempt to check the impact of Second Army assault by counter-attacks. To stabilize the situation in preparation for the armoured counter-attack.'

It can be seen from these assessments that to lay blame after the fact on the Allied intelligence services for not having a perfect impression of German positions at Omaha Beach would be frankly unjustified. Even if the 21st Army Group assessment had reached the assault divisions the day before the invasion it would not have changed their plans, their execution, or the outcome. Omaha Beach was a formidable challenge. It simply had to be taken if the Allies were to establish a cohesive and secure beachhead.

The German Coastal Defence Battery at Pointe du Hoc

The Pointe du Hoc is a dramatic promontory at the western end of Omaha sector. It lies some four miles from Vierville. Between the Vierville draw and Pointe du Hoc lies the Pointe et Raz de la Percee. These two 100-foot headlands look deceivingly similar from the sea. On the morning of 6 June this similarity would cause considerable confusion to one particular flotilla of the Royal Navy.

The 2nd Battalion of the United States Army Rangers had been tasked with the destruction of the formidable German battery at Pointe du Hoc , codenamed MAISEY. The force was carried in ten LCAs that were being guided by three small Royal Navy gunboats incorrectly toward the Pointe et Raz de la Percee. In the early morning twilight the navigation and identification of the target proved difficult until finally Colonel Rudder , commander of the Ranger assault force, realized the serious error that was being made and ordered his LCA to 'break ranks' and lead the force to the real objective. The currents, tide and errors of navigation made this assault force 40 minutes late. By that point it was daylight and surprise had been lost.

Neptune's planners had deemed the fortified Pointe 'key terrain' its capture vital to the landings at Omaha and Utah Beaches. It had been prioritized as Target No. 1 out of 300 enemy installations in the First US Army sector. This was because it had been transformed into a fortified 600x800 yards position housing six 155mm guns. These guns were each capable of firing a shell over 25,000 yards. Both Utah and Omaha Beaches were well within range. Once the fleet had closed on the beaches the ships and landing craft would also be in range of the guns. Two of the guns were already thought to be casemated while the others were housed in reinforced concrete bunkers. These had already proven highly resilient to air attack. The preliminary bombardments by the RAF and the Ninth US Army Air Force had commenced in early April and continued until the early morning of 6 June. The cratering and destruction caused by this relentless bombardment would have significant effect on the German commanders and the immediate area surrounding the blockhouses, damaging and disrupting the fort's defences, and more significantly shattering the cliff edge and cratering the rocky beach at the base of the cliffs. This destruction would subsequently prevent several of Rudder 's amphibious craft from getting into their designated positions on the assault run-in. The overall effects of this bombing will be considered in more detail in Chapter 3.

The battery had a 210-man garrison from the static 716th Coastal Defence Division. This consisted of about 125 men from the 726 Infantry Regiment and 85 artillery men from the 2nd Battery of the 1260th Coastal Artillery Regiment. The artillery company was responsible for manning the six 155mm guns which could engage targets out to a range of 20,000 metres including the coastal areas soon to be known as Omaha and Utah Beaches. The infantry garrison was tasked to protect the battery against ground assaults.

2nd Battalion the Rangers marching along the front at Weymouth, 1 June 1944, led by its commander Lieutenant Colonel James E. Rudder.

This threat was assessed as coming from inland. After all, no one would attempt to attack this natural fortress from the sea.

Training the V Corps for the Mission

The Rangers. The Greek historian Thucydides once wrote that 'We must remember that one man is much the same as another, and that he is best who is trained in the severest school.' The Rangers destined for the Omaha sector were certainly members of a highly trained and elite force. Their mission on D-Day demanded that they be at the height of physical fitness, in addition to being aggressive and independent. To meet the vigours ahead, they underwent a gruelling training programme in the Highlands of Scotland. There Lord Lovat's No. 4 Commando assisted the Rangers by putting them through a series of speed marches, assault course practices, unarmed combat lessons and cliff face assaults. With this foundation, the Rangers then moved to the Scottish coast where amphibious assaults were conducted on simulated defences and cliff positions. The culmination of this tough training programme took place in the south of England during April and May 1944. The Rangers then practised their impending assault on the cliffs on the Isle of White and near Swanage.

With the experience and advice from the British Commandos, the Rangers had developed various devices to help achieve their D-Day task. Each of their 10 LCAs were to be fitted with 3 pairs of rocket projectors mounted at the bow, amidships, and at the stern. The projectors could be initiated from a firing control system in the stern. When triggered, each pair of projectors would fire simultaneously dragging their payload up the cliff face. Each rocket pair could fire a grapnel hook attached to a ¾ inch plain rope, a toggle rope, or a rope ladder with wooden rungs every two feet. Each LCA would also carry a pair of smaller hand held rockets designed to be carried to the base of the objective and fired with a light rope attachment up to the cliff-top. Each craft also contained lightweight tubular extension ladders broken down for transit into four-foot lengths that could be quickly assembled and raised up the cliff face. To speed up the assembly process the assault troops pre-prepared 16-foot lengths using 4 foot sections. The Rangers training and experimentation process had led to the development of a set drill where the leading Ranger would climb to the top of the ladder and attach the next 16-foot length; that done, he would continue the climb until the cliff top could be reached. As a final option, four DUKWs were equipped with London Fire Brigade 100-foot extension ladders mounted in three folding sections. The ladders were also adapted to a more violent military use with a pair of Lewis machine guns fixed to the top of each of these ladders.

Thus equipped, this elite, highly trained force had to conduct what General Bradley considered the toughest task of any assault force on D-Day. As Bradley wrote in his memoir *A Soldiers Story* in 1951:

> *'...no soldier in my command has ever wished for a more difficult task than that which befell the 34 year old commander of this Provisional Ranger Force. Lieutenant Colonel James E. Rudder, a rancher from Brady, Texas, was to take a force of 200 men, land on a shingle shelf under the face of a 100 foot cliff, scale the cliff, and there destroy an enemy battery of coastal guns. "First time you mentioned it" Rudder recalls, "I thought you were trying to scare me".'*

After the war, Lt. Eikner of the 2nd Ranger Battalion gave an insightful testament on Rudder 's training methods:

> *'I can assure you, that when we went into battle after all this training there was no shaking of the knees or weeping or praying; we knew what we were getting into; we knew every one of us had volunteered for extra hazardous duty; we went into battle confident;*

*of course we were tense under fire, but we were intent on getting the
job done. We were actually looking forward to accomplishing our
mission.'*

Training the Assault Divisions

The 1st Division was the most experienced expeditionary
formation in the First Army. However, they, like the 29th Division,
had to attend the intense training course conducted at the Assault
Training Centre in Woolacombe. There they were drilled in the
tactics, techniques and procedures required to conduct opposed
beach landings, clear enemy strongpoints and operate with other
arms and services. The divisions then went on to conduct landing
training prior to participating in a series of exercises codenamed
'Fabius' at Slapton Sands in Devon. The Fabius exercises were dress
rehearsals for the actual invasion. Once the training was complete,
the assault forces moved to their marshalling areas. Captain Hall
takes up the story:

*'We were alerted on March 23rd 1944 to be ready for movement
to marshaling areas on short notice. We began relocation on May
7th and had completed this operation by the 10th of May. Once in the
marshaling areas we were sealed-in our assignments. The last few
days of May, we moved from the marshaling area to the ports for
embarkation. The 1st Division troops were loaded on board by the
3rd of June. Weymouth was my embarkation area. I was on board a
LCI as we left England.'*

The Assault Landing Plan

The V Corps mission was to secure a beachhead between Port-en-
Bessin in the East and the River Vire in the West. It would do so by
landing with two assault regiments or regimental combat teams
(RCTs) abreast, with the 16th RCT (1st Division) on the left, or East
flank, and 116th RCT (29th Division) on the right to the West. The
16th RCT was to go ashore at Easy Red , Fox Green, and Fox Red.
While the 116th on the right would land on Charlie, Dog Green, Dog
White, Dog Red, and Easy Green. Each regiment would use two
battalions in the first echelon, landing in columns of companies,
with the 3rd battalion landing team (BLT) in reserve behind them. A
total of nine companies and Company C, 2nd Rangers were to land
in the initial waves from 0630 hours. Off Pointe du Hoc, a follow-up
force of eight 65-man companies from the 2nd and 5th Rangers
would be standing by to support Colonel Rudder. However,

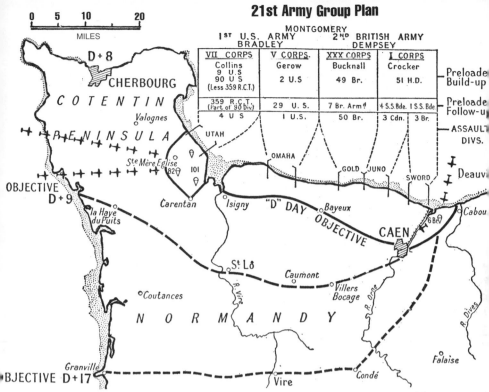

Rudder's signal to call this substantial force in to the Pointe would not be received, as a result Lieutenant Colonel Max F. Schneider (commanding the Provisional Ranger Force) would execute his alternate plan and take his force to the western end of Omaha Beach.

Amphibious Duplex-Drive (DD) Sherman tanks would provide an armoured spearhead for the eight assault companies. While the infantry and armour were engaging the German defences, about 300 combat engineers organized into breaching or gapping teams were to clear beach obstacles for the follow-on elements from V Corps. They were to land 10 minutes after the initial boats hit the beach. Their task was to cut a series of gaps through the 'petrified forest' of obstacles and mark them for follow-on craft. They would have to work fast before the rising tide (rising 20 feet on D-Day) covered many of the obstacles after only 30 minutes. The engineers would be supported by eight Sherman tanks from Company A, 743rd Tank Battalion fitted with bulldozer blades, each tank being capable of pushing obstacles out of a boat lane or crushing them into the sand.

Remaining rifle companies from the assault regiments would land between 0700-0730 hours, with support groups landing thereafter, including amphibious DUKW trucks that would be ferrying the artillery units ashore to provide initial intimate gunfire support to the assault troops.

Once a foothold had been established the assaulting infantry would clear the German defences covering the five prominent draws that offered the only vehicle routes off Omaha Beach. RCTs were to then push inland to battalion, regimental, and divisional objectives astride the N13 road from Caen to Isigny-sur-Mer. V Corps had the task of establishing a beachhead some four to six miles deep and fourteen miles wide.

Key regimental and battalion level tasks included securing objectives on the prominent ridge of high ground to the north of the River Aure. These planned D-Day objectives would act as blocking positions to the inevitable German counter-attacks. This extensive bridgehead would also provide V Corps with sufficient depth to build-up troop and logistic strength for subsequent operations and give security to the vulnerable landings of follow-on units during the early stages of the invasion. Behind this shield, Gerow would deploy his divisions, and link up with the Rangers at Pointe du Hoc. Another vital task would be to link up with the VII Corps, landing at Utah Beach around the elbow of the Cotentin peninsula. This mission fell to the 29th Division. The 115th Infantry Regiment, under the command of Colonel Eugene N. Slappey, was ordered as late as 3rd June 1944, to include Isigny sur Mer amongst its D-Day objectives. This would be an essential prelude to linking up with VII Corps somewhere between the Rivers Vire and the Douve between the towns of Carentan and Isigny. On the eastern V Corps flank, the 1st Division would need to link-up with the British to the West of Port en Bessin before the Corps pushed inland toward St-Lô and Caumont. The V Corps advance would then be staged to conform to the advance of General Miles Dempsey's British Second Army on the left.

To achieve these ambitious goals the overall concept of operations for V Corps was to establish itself in Normandy by D+15 in four general stages:

First Stage: The initial assault phase by Force 'O', consisted of the reinforced 1st Division with elements from 29th Division and the Provisional Ranger Force, in addition to Corps artillery, armour, engineer and service attachments. This force totalled 34,142 men and 3,306 vehicles.

Second Stage: Force 'B' was the follow-up force consisting of

25,115 men and 4,429 vehicles. This included the rest of the 29th Division . Force 'B' was scheduled to arrive off the beach after noon on D-Day.

Third Stage: The pre-loaded build-up contingent consisted of 17,500 men and 2,300 vehicles. This element was to arrive on D+1 and D+2. It would include the 2nd Division.

Fourth Stage: The final component included 32,000 troops and 9,446 vehicles that were to land between D+2 and D+15. Many of these elements were attached to V Corps for movement only and did not constitute part of the Corps order of battle.

In the first stage the Corps concept of operations was to assault across Omaha Beach with the reinforced 'Big Red One.' General Clarence C. Huebner, commanding the veteran 1st Division, would conduct the initial assault with two additional regiments, the 115th and 116th, from the unblooded 29th Division under command. The plan was designed to allow a rapid transition from an assault by a single division into a two-division advance abreast into the hinterland. It was believed that this plan would provide the necessary unity of command during the early critical stages of the assault.

On orders from General Gerow commander of V Corps, Major General Charles H. Gerhardt would come ashore, regroup and resume command of the 29th. To facilitate this early phase and the subsequent transition, the plan required Brigadier General Norman D. Cota assistant divisional commander of the 29th to land with his leading regiment. General Cota was to come ashore with the 116th, and thereby help General Huebner handle these units until Gerow could order Gerhardt ashore sometime in the afternoon of D-Day to set-up his divisional headquarters in France. Cota and his staff were called the '29th Division Advanced Headquarters' by the Corps Headquarters. Unofficially this provisional command was known as the 'bastard brigade'.

General Norman Cota was a remarkable officer. In late May he had briefed the Divisional Staff in the 29th Division Headquarters on what they could expect. He captured the reality of D-Day with astonishing prescience. He said to the assembled group:

> *'This is different from any of the other exercises that you've had so far. The little discrepancies that we tried to correct on Slapton Sands are going to be magnified and are*

75

General Norman Cota

going to give way to incidents that you might first view as chaotic. The air and naval bombardment and the artillery support are reassuring. But you're going to find confusion. The landing craft aren't going in on schedule and people are going to be landed in the wrong place. Some won't be landing at all. The enemy will try, and will have some success, in preventing our gaining a lodgment. But we must improvise, carry on, not lose our heads. Nor must we add to the confusion.'

In fact, Cota did not like the plan for Omaha Beach. He had wanted to land in darkness to minimize the effects of the German defences. For him, the advantages of surprise and concealment outweighed the risk of chaos as boats manoeuvred in the darkness. He was not alone in voicing his concerns.

Cota would emerge from D-Day as one of the legendary figures responsible for encouraging and cajoling the men up the bluffs. He would lead one particular group off the beach and then guide them through fire and manoeuvre and house-clearing drills before finally returning to the beach down the Vierville draw to galvanize the rest of the 29th Division still fixed on the beach!

Another prominent critic of the V Corps plan was Major General Charles Corlett who had been sent from the Pacific Theatre to Britain to impart his experiences as a divisional commander in the amphibious assault on Kwajalein atoll. He recalled briefing a British audience on amphibious techniques in use at Kwajalein only to receive this extraordinary response from a senior British officer: 'If we have an island to take, you ought to do it'.

Unfortunately the Allies appear to have been culturally incapable, or too dogmatic, to consider the lessons learned by the expeditionary forces conducting MacArthur's island-hopping campaign. This was highlighted when Corlett asked General Eisenhower and Bradley why the first wave at Omaha was to land in conventional, highly vulnerable landing craft instead of the new amphibious armoured vehicles or Landing Vehicles Tracked ('Alligators'). Corlett later wrote that he was 'squelched' for his trouble and made to feel that the Pacific was a 'bush league' campaign. Alligators could well have altered the outcome for the first wave. Moving at up to 18 miles per hour across the beach, these vehicles would have given the assault troops sufficient speed and protection to allow the bombardment to continue for longer, while also minimizing early casualties caused by small arms fire.

CHAPTER THREE

THE INVASION

The Allied Invasion Machine

By 26th May the assault troops had completed their intensive training and were now moving from their concentration areas to the marshalling sites near the ports of embarkation. There they were sealed into fenced camps. Detailed briefings commenced four days before they were ordered to form up into ship and assault craft loads. Until then only commanding officers and one officer in each unit had been briefed on the actual plan of attack. Now company commanders were notified and at D-3 the junior officers and NCOs were briefed.

Then units were broken up into their assault groups. Great efforts had been made to ensure that every man knew his task during the initial assault and during the immediate follow-up phase. A mass of intricately detailed models, photographs, maps and even simulations were used, exact in every available detail, but bearing codenames rather than actual place names. Even at this late stage

GIs embarking on their LCIs prior to the cross Channel run to the Normandy coast.

the troops were not told of their destination until they had got aboard their ships. Tight security was essential if the invasion was not to be stalled on the beaches of Normandy. Once aboard their assault craft the actual maps of the beach areas would be issued and confirmatory briefings given.

General Eisenhower now faced the moment of truth. He must now issue the orders to launch this vast operation. As D-Day drew near he met with his principal commanders and staff on a daily then twice daily basis to consider the weather forecasts. May had been consistently fine and now the greatest expeditionary operation in history was threatened by a deteriorating weather picture. Eisenhower courageously postponed D-Day from the 5th to the 6th June.

In reporting his decision to the Combined Chiefs, General Eisenhower said that approaching bad weather might prevent vital air and airborne operations. He added that a second delay of 24 hours might well be necessary, but that any further postponement would have very serious consequences – not least the security of the entire operation. Beyond the 7th June time and tides would no longer be right and troops and equipment would all have to be released back to the insecure concentration areas. The whole complex process of mounting the operation would have to be repeated.

Convoys already at sea were ordered to reverse course and go to sheltered anchorages. Unfortunately one convoy had missed the postponement signal. It included 128 LCTs, 9 escorts and a rescue tug. By 0900 hours on 4th June it was 25 miles south of the Isle of Wight heading for France. Within the hour aircraft had turned the convoy back. By the time the ships had reached Weymouth Bay the Channel was being whipped-up by a gale.

At the evening meeting on 4th June Group Captain Stagg could offer some improvement for the morning of the 6th. General Eisenhower now held to his previous decision that D-Day would be the 6th June, but he would confirm or alter this at the 0400 hours meeting on 5th June. However, if the assault was to take place on the 6th Admiral Ramsey had to order the more distant convoys to sea at once.

Consider what can best be described as the 'loneliness of command' when the buck stops with you and you alone. Spare a thought for Eisenhower at 0930 hours on Monday 5th June with a storm blowing down outside and his air advisors advocating a

further delay. Neptune-Overlord would involve nearly 3 million men. Its success and their fate rested solely on Eisenhower's decision. With the indomitable words 'OK, let 'er rip', General Eisenhower launched the operation.

The Sea Passage

Early on the 5th June the first groups of the Neptune assault force sailed from their sheltered ports and before the day was far advanced, a steady stream of 1,213 warships and 4,126 landing craft was proceeding to sea. As one reporter wrote of this spectacle 'They came, rank after relentless rank, ten lanes wide, twenty miles across, five thousand ships of every description.' By the evening of 5th June the minesweepers had cleared the way through the German barriers, in spite of heavy seas and strong tides making exact navigation difficult. In mid-Channel a mine-cleared rendezvous had been prepared codenamed 'Picadilly Circus.' From there the five landing groups, Forces Utah, Omaha, Gold, Juno and Sword proceeded towards their objectives. As the early morning progressed at 0251 hours, about 11-12 miles off the French coast, the assault troops left the comparative comfort and security of the transports and loaded into their appointed assault craft that were

bouncing like corks in a bottle. Many of the soldiers were already weakened by seasickness. With a heavy swell and 3-4 foot waves the assault troops now faced a long and dangerous run-in. Instead of adapting to local conditions many naval commanders rigidly stuck to their orders with disastrous consequences for many craft and most particularly the inherently unseaworthy amphibious tanks. At H-50 minutes 32 tanks from two companies were launched and in quick succession 27 went to the bottom, swamped by waves or with their screens shattered by the pounding seas. Only 5 of these hapless vehicles would make it to shore where three of them were quickly destroyed by German anti-tank guns. A similar disaster befell the DUKWs carrying the 105-mm artillery guns, crew and ammunition intended to provide fire support to the first waves ashore. While this tragedy was unfolding the strong coastal current was pushing the assault craft to the left a factor that would add to the confusion on the beach.

Chief Yeoman William Garwood Bacon, USN Reserve (Ret) recalled his experiences as he headed for Normandy:

'In an overcrowded port, we clambered aboard the USS LCI designated by the Army as USS LCI(L)-531. We were assigned to the number 3 hold, numbers 1, 2, and 4 being occupied by Army

Chief Yeoman William Garwood Bacon, USN Reserve

personnel. Once aboard, no one was permitted ashore for security reasons. We had been informed that we would not be in the harbour more than three days. Our quarters consisted simply of bunks stacked four high in rows so close together that it was impossible to go between them while clad in battle togs. As we scrambled down the ladder, we shrugged out of our packs, gas masks and ammunition carriers and carried them in our hands along with our weapons, in order to squeeze back to our assigned bunk. We felt reasonably certain we would be there for a couple of days anyway, so everyone settled his mind to that fact.

From June 1 until the afternoon of June 4, we spent our time playing cards, reading, passing rumours, eating our K, C, and D rations in shifts up on the open deck, and waiting to use the limited supply of water in the two wash basins on the ship. Considering that so many men were crowded with their equipment into such a small space, there was little or no bickering or arguing. On the morning of June 4, a Sunday, services were held on the open decks. Few if any failed to whisper a solemn 'Amen' to the prayers for guidance and protection in the great undertaking which we were about to experience.

On June 5 at 1700 our flotilla of LCIs got underway. We were permitted to remain above decks until blackout time. As far as I could see, on both sides of the ship as well as fore and aft, there were ships, ships and more ships.

Despite all that lay ahead, we somehow were able to sleep after our boat commander read us Eisenhower's speech. Some of the ship's crew gave occasional reports of huge armadas of airplanes passing overhead toward the French coast for the apparent purpose of softening up the 'Jerries.'

Around 0600 on June 6, the big guns of the Allied fleet began a mighty barrage on the invasion coast. Shortly afterwards, we began filing topside again for our morning ration of food. We all ate something because no one knew when we would eat again. Everything seemed to be going smoothly and very few of us inexperienced men could shake off the feeling that this was just another manoeuvre. Around 0630 the Allied sea monsters, belching forth their message of death, suddenly ceased firing as abruptly as they had begun. We dipped our mess kits in the cold greasy water in an effort to clean them, and took another hasty glance at the smoking and blazing shoreline, and ducked through the hatchway leading down to our quarters.

According to our schedule, our craft was to land on Dog White Beach at H+100 minutes (0810) through a fifty-yard passage cleared by our demolition men. Our ship's crew were veterans of North Africa, Sicily, and Salerno and promised us they would get us ashore somehow. At 0755, with only fifteen minutes left before our scheduled landing, no shots had been fired on us and we were rapidly approaching what seemed and proved to be an impassable barrier. Nowhere in sight was the promised cleared passage.'

Ray Lambert was a young Staff Sergeant in a medical section with the 2nd Battalion, 16th Infantry RCT. His job was to get his men ashore in the first wave and find a suitable place for an 'aid station'. His account captures the atmosphere and experience of that long approach to the beach:

'After we left Weymouth to cross the Channel I spent time going over the map that I had of the beach where we were to land. I had been briefed and had seen a sand table 'mock up' of the beach area. During the crossing – to see so many ships and boats of every size and shape was unbelievable. There were thousands so close that at times you could hear the men talking on the next boat. Every ship and craft was packed with men. Some of the smaller craft were having a hard time staying afloat in the very heavy weather. Many men were seasick...

The 16th Infantry Regiment of the 1st Division was the only 'first wave' assault unit on D-Day with combat experience. It didn't help much. I had been with the 16th in North Africa in 1942 and in Sicily in 1943. Nothing I had seen in all those battles would compare with what we encountered at 'Easy Red' on June 6, 1944.

I was sick from the time I was loaded into the Higgins boat from

the LCI as was everyone else. There were so many men throwing up all over the boat and each other that we could hardly stand. The boat to our left got hit and burst into flames. Many of the men on that boat were on fire. All that could went overboard. I remember one was burning all over – even his shoes were burning. Those who got into the water were drawn under by the weight of their equipment and never seen again. There were so many craft and with the seas running from 4 to six feet the entire wave that I was in was drifting away from where we were to have landed. The boat on our right blew up and most of the troops on board were killed.

Ray Lambert

We were under intense fire from machine guns, rifles, mortars and artillery all from both flanks as well as from dead ahead. Our heavy gun support from the battleships was halted because they could not tell how far our troops had advanced. We could hear the machine gun shells hitting the ramp and side of our boat. We (I) knew when we lowered the ramp we would walk into a death trap, but there was no other way. Those support Navy vessels that could fire sent shells so close over our heads that we could hear the shells pass and I am sure I felt the wind from a few. We continued to get enemy fire from 105's, 88's, 40mm mortars and machine guns. The enemy had mined the area and these mines were exploding. It was indescribable. I said to Cpl. Herbert Meyer, "If there is a hell this has to be it". I was so sick that I didn't care if I died. I just wanted to get off that damn boat. There were so many dead and wounded in the water that our boat was going over them. The DD tanks were going right to the bottom as they drove off the ramp from their craft. Many of the tank crews went down with the tank. Some crewmembers did get out and were floating in the water.

As we neared the beach I saw all the obstacles and wondered how any of us would ever reach the beach... '

The Coastal Bombardment

At 0550 hours just before dawn on the 6th June gigantic flickering tongues of flame on the horizon told the assault divisions that the bombardment force had commenced the task of engaging the enemy coastal defences in the Omaha sector. Brief duels occurred as German batteries responded. The Pointe du Hoc remained strangely silent. The air armada overhead was similarly engaged with its vital air and airborne tasks. The fleet had watched in silence as thousands of aircraft passed overhead throughout the night. No shots were fired. The fleet had been forbidden to engage aircraft during this approach to the continent after the disastrous friendly fire incidents in Sicily the year before.

At 0600 hours 480 B-24 liberator bombers from the American 8th Air Force dropped 1,285 tons of bombs on 13 targets. In poor visibility bombs were dropped late and this deadly payload landed harmlessly 3 miles inland. Much of the German defence at Omaha Beach was now alert and unscathed by the preparatory fire.

Approaching the Beach

Fred Hall Jr. was the S-3 with the 2nd Battalion 16th Infantry Regiment. The Battalion was scheduled to land in the Easy Red sector of Omaha Beach at H-Hour 0630 hours. Fred Hall was to land as part of the battalion advanced command post along with his Commanding Officer Lieutenant Colonel Herbert Hicks, the Executive Officer (XO) and other key staff officers and NCOs. He recalled:

'We reached our rendezvous area before daylight, 15,000 to

French coast in sight: 'The Sea was choppy and we had poor visibility... some in the boat were sick'.

20,000 metres off the beach. The weather was low overcast and the sea was rough. We went over the side of USS Henrico to load into our LCVP's. After loading, we formed in a circle near our ship before heading toward shore... The Sea was choppy and we had poor visibility. Some in the boat were sick. We could see the battleships and cruisers stretched out parallel to the beach as they fired their

Fred Hall

guns. Closer in I saw for the first time, rocket craft releasing their rockets. We could hear aircraft overhead but the clouds were too low to see them.'

Fred Hall, like so many other men in the 1st Division, had taken part in the landings in North Africa ('Torch') and Sicily ('Husky'). However this was to be his first daylight landing.

During the run-in Bill Friedman recalled 'seeing the DD tanks being launched and trying to make headway in the rough seas. It was terrible to watch. They just went to the bottom.' Many veterans spoke of seeing several dinghies containing men in lifejackets during the long run-in to the beach. These were the handful of survivors from the drowned DD tanks. The landing craft could not stop and pick them up, they were left to their fate unless the designated rescue boats found them later. A friend and acquaintance of Bill Friedman was already ahead of him during the run-in. His name was Robert Capa the already legendary war photographer. Capa had spent a difficult night on board USS *Chase* trying to decide whether he should accompany one of the assault companies from the 2nd Battalion or go in with Colonel Robert Taylor's Regimental Headquarters after the first waves of infantry. He wrote in his memoir *Slightly Out of Focus*:

'On the one hand, the objectives of Company B looked interesting, and to go along with them seemed to be a pretty safe bet. Then again, I used to know Company E very well and the story I had got with them in Sicily was one of the best during the war. I was about to choose between Companies B and E when Colonel Taylor... tipped me off that regimental headquarters would follow close behind the first waves of infantry. If I went with him, I wouldn't miss the action, and I'd be a little safer. This sounded like a real favourite – an even money bet – two to one to be alive in the evening... I was a gambler. I decided to go in with Company E in the first wave.'

For the young men in the V Corps there would be no such choice of which wave to join. Each man had an assigned task and a position in the assault craft. There would be no shirking of responsibilities for the men who would lead the 'Great Crusade.'

CHAPTER FOUR

THE RANGERS AT POINTE DU HOC
Tour A

Route to Pointe du Hoc

The Pointe du Hoc may be approached from the N.13 (Isigny – Bayeux – Caen). **Leave the N.13** half way between La Cambe and Osmanvile on the **D.199** and go north to Grandcamp-Maisy. Drive into the Centre of town and arrive at the pretty fishing port with its active dockside fish market and restaurants. Stop and identify the German Atlantic Wall bunkers. Drive around the quayside to the right, or East, to the sea front (*Quai Crampon*). On the right hand corner of the road there are memorials to elements of Heavy Group, Bomber Command and Sergeant Frank Peregory, Congressional Medal of Honor winner in 29th Division. He had single-handedly destroyed a German machine gun nest that had held up the Divisional advance on Grandcamp on 8 June. His citation noted that his action 'was directly responsible for the advance of the Battalion and enabled it to take its objective, Grandcamp.' Sadly Sergeant Peregory was killed in

The bombardment force commenced the task of engaging the enemy coastal defences in the Omaha sector. Warships off the coastline had commenced firing at 0550 hours, just before dawn.

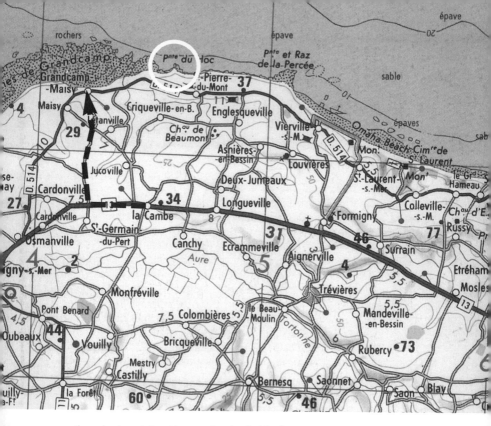

action six days later. He now lies buried in St Laurent.

Further along the promenade is the Ranger Museum. **Follow the D.514** in the direction of Pointe du Hoc and Vierville-sur-Mer. You may detour briefly to the South to visit Criqueville-en-Bessin where there is a memorial to the American Rangers in the XIIIth century village church. Return to the D.514 by following the D.204 North towards the coast. At the **junction in St. Pierre du Mont, turn left** and follow the prominent signs into the Pointe du Hoc car park. The large car park is equipped with restrooms and informative display boards explaining the events at Pointe du Hoc and one board describing the *Sentier du Littoral* footpath from Vierville to Grandcamp

The route to the memorial from the D.514 is now named Ranger Road. In 1944 it was a narrow road controlled by a guard post halfway along its length. Encircling the battery position were deep, barbed wire fences and minefields that were covered by observation and fire from the numerous, carefully sited inner trenches and outposts. The memorial site occupies an area of over 30 acres. Since 1979 the American Battle Monuments Commission and the Comité De la Pointe Du Hoc have administered it. It is now preserved and maintained by the American Battle Monuments Commission following a hand over ceremony from the French Comité de la Pointe du Hoc attended by General Omar Bradley, on 6 June 1979. There is a granite memorial symbolizing a commando dagger atop the German

Above: Ranger Memorial
Below: Effects of concentrated bombardment at Pointe du Hoc.

Entrance to the Command Bunker at Pointe du Hoc.

The Pointe from the east.

observation bunker at the Pointe. An inscribed granite plinth bears the following inscription in English and French: 'TO THE HEROIC RANGER COMMANDOES D 2 RN E 2 RN F2 RN OF THE 116TH INF WHO UNDER THE COMMAND OF COLONEL JAMES E. RUDDER OF THE FIRST AMERICAN DIVISION ATTACKED AND TOOK POSSESSION OF THE POINTE DU HOC'.

Park in the well laid-out car park and walk along the evident footpath past the gun towards the sea. You will now be able to see the extent of this position and its formidable and inherent strength. This was a grim target for any ground assault. Now walk to the German observation bunker and Ranger Memorial on the point itself and find a suitable viewpoint on the bunker roof to examine the coastline. Look right or east along the cliffs and identify the Pointe et Raz de la Percée some 5 kilometres away. Look down onto the rocky beach and identify the 500-metre stretch where the Rangers landed. Look to the west and identify Grandcamp-Maisy, the obvious town along the coast, and beyond that the Cotentin Peninsula and Utah Beach which is due west of you.

The Rangers Approach the Objective

The original plan for the assault on the Pointe du Hoc declared that the assault was to be led by Rudder's (XO) or second in command. This very much rankled with the Colonel, who rightly felt that he should lead his men into battle. Fate played a hand in seeing that he would get his wish. Just prior to sailing for France the battalion XO got thoroughly drunk aboard the transport ship in Weymouth harbour. Rudder had to send him ashore where he was promptly hospitalized, and assume both the leadership and overall command of the assault by D, E, and F companies on the Pointe. He notified General Huebner of the change of plan. Astonishingly Huebner felt that Rudder was too valuable to 'risk getting knocked out in the very first round.' To this Rudder retorted:

Colonel Max Schneider led the Provisional Ranger Force that was to relieve Colonel Rudder

'I'm sorry, sir, I'm going to have to disobey you. If I don't take it, it may not go.'

As events were to prove this was indeed a fortunate twist of fate.

The rangers crossed to France in HMS

Pointe du Hoc under attack prior to D-Day.

Amsterdam, Ben My Chree, and USS LCT 46 which carried the DUKWs and their crews. Once in position off the French coast, the assault force transferred into their landing craft.

Rudder's flotilla of ten landing craft and four DUKWs now had a twelve-mile final approach to the objective. In darkness and in rough seas they advanced under the guidance of a Royal Navy Fairmile motor launch (ML) and two British LCS (LCS 91 and LCS 102). During this final approach the grim conditions inflicted the first casualties on Rudder's men. En route from their transport area, the vessels were shipping so much water that all hands had to bail with their helmets. Unfortunately, LCA914, a supply craft sank, with all but one of its crew. Rudder had now lost a vital supply of reserve ammunition and other equipment. The next tragedy occurred when LCA 860 sank from under 20 men and the company commander from D Company. They were rescued. The remaining force of nine

LCAs and four DUKWs now struggled on towards the dark, featureless coastline.

The next incident was to have a considerable impact on Rudder's plan of enveloping the point from its two coastal flanks. The Royal Navy guide boat ML 304 had become disorientated during the run-in. Lieutenant Eikner, Rudder's communications officer, subsequently described what happened in a letter written to *After the Battle* in 1994:

'When daylight dawned, it was apparent to Colonel Rudder that we were off course and heading directly towards Pointe et Raz de la Percée some three miles east of Pointe du Hoc (which was to be attacked from the land-ward side by Company C, 2nd Rangers). Colonel Rudder, in our lead craft, literally forced his boat to break ranks and flank west. The infuriated British officer doing the navigating thought we were trying to abort the mission and tried to run Colonel Rudder's craft down; he soon realized his mistake, however. This error of navigation changed the course of the whole battle and caused us to arrive at Pointe du Hoc 38 minutes late, thereby triggering the option that took the ranger Main Force to Omaha Beach where they were supposed to pass through the lines of the 116th Infantry and then fight on down to Pointe du Hoc on the double. We expected them to arrive by noon but they did not arrive until noon on the third day, after we had been counter-attacked five times and had suffered casualties of 70 per cent.'

The navigation error had other implications for Rudder 's men. The force now had to traverse the four kilometres of coastline under fire from cliff top gun positions. The next casualty was a DUKW struck by 20mm cannon fire. Then LCS 91 ran into difficulties in the heavy seas and was holed below the water line by German machine gun fire, sinking shortly thereafter, but not before its skipper, Lieutenant N. E. Fraser RNVR returned fire with the craft's .5 Vickers machine gun.

At about this time the G3 (operations) watch-keeper of 1st Infantry Division Headquarters on board the USS *Ancon* wrote in the divisional journal 'a brilliant white flare seen near Pointe du Hoc.' The German garrison was now fully alert and expecting an amphibious assault. At this stage Rudder may have considered the response his plan had first received from Admiral Hall's Intelligence Officer during the preparatory phase back in England: 'It can't be done. Three old women with brooms could keep the Rangers from climbing that cliff'.

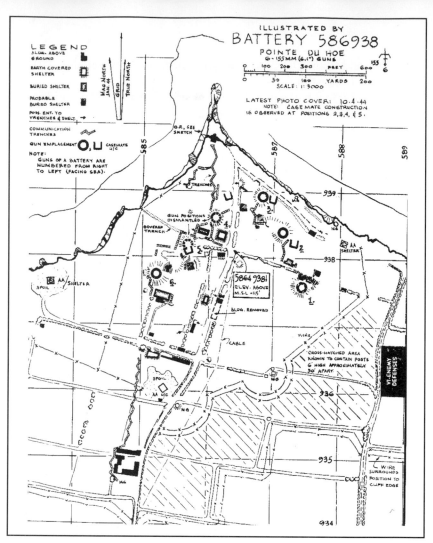

Map of Pointe du Hoc from the original Operations Order. Note the spelling error in the title.

In full daylight the boats grounded at 0708 hours. Any hope of dividing the attention of the defences by attacking from both sides of the point had gone as all craft beached on the eastern side of the promontory on a 500-metre frontage. On board *USS Satterlee* the ship's crew could clearly see the German garrison preparing to 'repel boarders' from the cliff top. Then at 0710 hours the *Satterlee* came under fire from a pillbox at the Pointe; the destroyer engaged the offending German gun. This also had the effect of dispersing some of the Germans on top of the cliffs and giving the Rangers sufficient respite to commence their scaling operations.

The COMDESDIV 36 action report was written contemporaneously based on message traffic and observer reports. At 0710 it states:

> ' the first boat of the 2nd Rangers... to attack Pointe du Hoe [sic] landed... to the east of the Pointe. These boats were forty minutes late in arriving... six out of the ten boats foundered... between one... and two... hundred yards from the beach. Most of the Rangers... reached the beach.' Five minutes later the action report went on to say: 'The fortifications at Pointe du Hoe [sic] had been under heavy fire... to H minus 05 minutes. However this fire had been lifted according to schedule and when the Rangers landed fortyfive [sic] minutes later the Germans had filtered back into the fortifications and were waiting for them with machine guns, mortars, rifles and hand grenades... As the Rangers landed they found themselves pinned under the cliffs and were being rapidly cut to pieces... . I immediately ordered SATTERLEE to close the point and take the cliff tops under... fire... Her fire control was excellent and the Rangers were able to establish a foothold on the cliff top.'

At 0728 the naval shore fire control party under Lt. P. C. Johnson USNR reached the cliff top and established communications with *Satterlee*. As Johnson moved away from the cliffs advancing inland with the Rangers he ensured that the Rangers established communications with the destroyer using light signals. COMDESDIV 36 noted that:

> 'by this means SATTERLEE and later THOMPSON and HARDING were able to repel several enemy counter-attacks which otherwise would have wiped out this Ranger Battalion... The gallant fight of... our Rangers against tremendous odds and difficulties was an inspiration to all naval personnel fortunate enough to witness this phase of the battle. The Rangers were magnificent.'

At 0900 all destroyers from DESRON 18 were ordered to close on the coast across the Omaha sector and assist the troops to breach the defences. Their intervention would prove decisive. At Pointe du Hoc the *USS Satterlee* was picking off enemy gun positions. USS *McCook* also logged that she had knocked one gun off the cliffs and that another gun had been blown up into the air. Naval gunfire was to be a vital component in Rudder 's defence of the Pointe over the next 48 hours as his ever-dwindling garrison came under repeated fire and counter-attacks by German troops from the 716th and 352nd Divisions.

Securing the Fortress

So while the main assault was underway on Omaha Beach, D, E, and F companies of the 2nd Ranger Battalion were engaged in their isolated action three miles to the west of Vierville. With so many setbacks it is remarkable to stand on the cliffs today beside the German bunkers and realize that Colonel Rudder would still achieve his mission after such an appalling start.

With the *Satterlee* sweeping the cliff top with fire forcing many Germans to ground, other defenders stood their ground in exposed positions and engaged the Rangers as they crossed the 30 metre strip of shingle between the waters edge and the base of the cliffs. The German troops tossed grenades down the cliff face onto the beach and engaged the fleeting targets below with rifle and machine gunfire. During this exposed crossing, 15 men were wounded by automatic fire from a machine gun nest along the cliff top 200 metres to the east of the point.

The *Fairmile* ML-304 crew now joined the battle and engaged the Germans with machine gun fire. While this duel was taking place the Rangers fired their rocket projectors up the cliff face. All but one of the LCAs managed to get at least one line up to the cliff edge. The hand held rockets were also fired providing more routes up, meanwhile other Rangers assembled their portable ladders and took advantage of a 40 foot mound of clay and rock that had collapsed in front of Rudder's landing craft during the initial naval bombardment. From this mound which still exists, a 16-foot ladder and toggle rope provided another route to the top. Small groups of Rangers now swarmed up the cliff and found cover at the top in the shell holes and craters made by the VIII and IX Army Air Force pre-D-Day bomber raids. Additional cover had also been created by the blast effects of the 250 fourteen inch shells fired on the battery by the USS *Texas* during the early morning of 6th June.

Within 5 minutes the first Ranger had reached the top and within 15 minutes all of E Company from LCA 888 had climbed up and were fanning out to clear the Germans from their fortified positions. The official American account described the subsequent events as a 'wild and frenzied scene'. Meanwhile Colonel Rudder was establishing his initial command post at the base of the cliff in a shallow cave.

At the water's edge the DUKWs were unable to get up onto the rocky ledge and approach the cliffs due in part to the cratering (still

Small teams of Rangers were in action defending their holdings on the Pointe from German counter-attacks.

visible at low tide) caused by the devastating sea and air barrage. On one DUKW Ranger Sergeant Stivison extended his British Merryweather ladder 90 feet into the air and manned his twin Lewis guns as planned. The distance from the cliffs was too great for the ladder to reach and with the action of the waves taking effect on the partly grounded DUKW, Stivison found himself swaying uncontrollably from side to side. Astonishingly he still managed to keep his balance and fire the guns in the general direction of the enemy.

At 0725 lieutenant Eikner transmitted the code-word indicating 'men up the cliff' on his SCR 300 radio, over the Ranger Command frequency. The Ranger control station acknowledged this message. At 0745 he transmitted the message 'Praise the Lord' denoting that all men were now up the cliff. This message went unacknowledged. By this time Colonel Rudder had moved his command post up the cliff and sited it between the collapsed cliff edge and a destroyed anti-aircraft gun emplacement at the eastern edge of the enemy battery position. From there, Rudder could only wait while his well-trained, highly independent soldiers fought their small unit actions with the remaining German garrison. When manpower permitted, small groups of Rangers were dispatched out from the command post to clear snipers and groups of enemy from their positions. This task would continue throughout the day.

Three hundred metres west of the German observation bunker an anti-aircraft gun position maintained a sporadic harassing fire on the Rangers throughout the morning. At 0740 a group of twelve Rangers had been tasked to destroy this gun, however, German automatic fire and mortars routed their attack. Moments later this party was overwhelmed by a German counter-attack. One man escaped to recount the disaster. The Ranger command post was only 100 metres from this action but the ground was so torn up and the battlefield so confused that the command group knew nothing until the survivor returned. Another attack was quickly initiated on this enemy position. This time the dozen Rangers and a mortar team were caught halfway to the objective by artillery fire and nearly all of them were killed or wounded. Later that day one burst of fire from that enemy position actually caught Rudder and wounded him in the left leg. Fortunately the bullet missed the bone and passed right through his flesh. Rudder kept fighting. Another machine gun position at the eastern end of the position also held out for most of the morning until it was finally dispatched by naval gunfire that blew the cliff top and the enemy position into the sea.

While the battle for the battery position raged on Rudder 's force was continuing to lose men and ammunition. However, one unexpected individual reinforcement did turn up and join the Rangers. Sergeant Leonard Goodgal of the 506 Parachute Infantry Regiment, 101st Airborne Division, had landed in France during the night and found himself close to Pointe du Hoc. Hearing the battle he 'marched to the sound of the guns' and joined Rudder's beleaguered force.

The Guns are Found

Walk back along Ranger Road and **cross the Grandcamp-Vierville Road** and look south into the field. Facing south and just off to your right, you will be able to see a fence line with hedging running in a straight line away from the main road. **Follow the line of the fence** and you will come to the next large oblong field with a few scattered trees in it. It was in this former apple orchard that the guns were located and destroyed by the Rangers. Beyond the field you will see the original farm complex. By coincidence, on 9th June 1944, General Bradley's first command post was

Track to the position of the concealed guns south of Pointe du Hoc.

established in France in this very orchard.

Return to the Pointe du Hoc via the hamlet of Le Guay and complete your visit to the memorial site.

While some of Rudder's men set about clearing the German bunkers, about 36 men from D and E Company moved through the battery position to the Grandcamp-Vierville road at Le Guay sometime between 0800 and 0830. Shortly thereafter another dozen Rangers from F Company reached the road and linked up with the

A 155mm gun of the type at Pointe du Hoc. When they were eventually discovered they were rendered useless using thermite grenades.

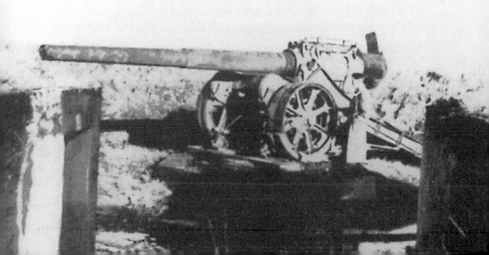

larger party. A roadblock and defensive perimeter was established both on and beyond the road. The Rangers now awaited the link-up force from V Corps, unaware of the disaster occurring a few miles to their East at Omaha Beach.

Meanwhile as small groups of Rangers attacked individual German bunkers and positions it became clear that something was very wrong. The casemates were all empty. The guns were not in the battery position. Rudimentary decoys were found, consisting of wooden telegraph poles. The whole operation appeared to have been a wasted effort.

In 1984 Ranger Sergeant Len Lommell explained in an ITN interview that the Germans 'were bombed silly with thousands and thousands of bombs from aerial bombardment and ships also, so they moved their guns in anticipation, maybe weeks before D-Day – and to an alternative position.' In fact the guns had been moved on 3rd June into an apple orchard south of the Grandcamp-Vierville road.

From 0900 patrols were dispatched to check the immediate vicinity for the guns. Lommell was part of a two-man patrol that went along a track from the main road. After going about 200 metres he found the missing guns. He described the moment of discovery:

'And there they were, in camouflaged positions pointing towards Utah Beach, with all their shells and everything in readiness to be fired, and their men, about one hundred or so Germans in a field, being reorganized by their leaders and listening to their officers. I went down into the emplacement and took my thermite grenades and laid them in the hinges and traversing mechanism, anything that could be melted by a thermite grenade, to make it inoperable.'

Short of grenades, he smashed the gun sights with his rifle butt while his companion stood guard. When Lommell and his partner left the guns a second patrol arrived and added to the destruction, using additional thermite grenades. In a relatively brief moment the guns had been rendered useless and Colonel Rudder had achieved his primary mission.

The Siege Begins

Within the Pointe du Hoc battery position the Germans were now recovering from their initial shock and confusion. Isolated German pockets now kept up a steady resistance. Counter-attacks were improvised. About an hour after the assault had begun the

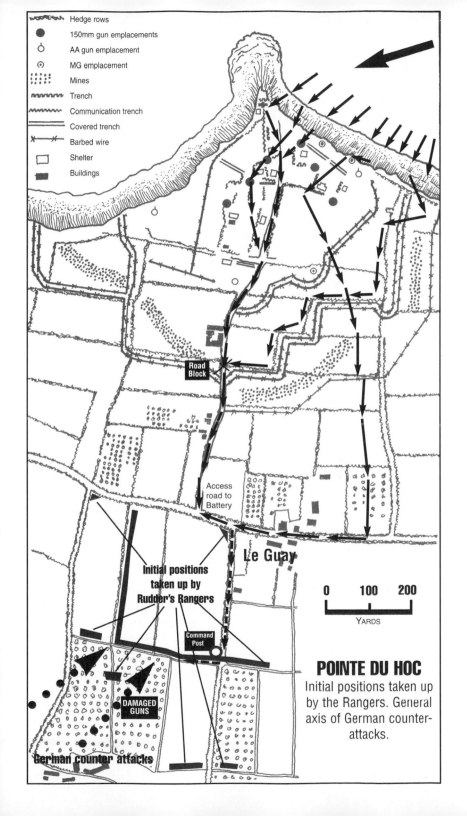

Hedge rows

● 150mm gun emplacements

○ AA gun emplacement

⊙ MG emplacement

⋮⋮⋮ Mines

〰 Trench

〜 Communication trench

══ Covered trench

✕✕✕ Barbed wire

▭ Shelter

▬ Buildings

Road Block

Access
road to
Battery

Le Guay

**Initial positions
taken up by
Rudder's Rangers**

**Command
Post**

0   100   200

YARDS

POINTE DU HOC
Initial positions taken up
by the Rangers. General
axis of German counter-
attacks.

**DAMAGED
GUNS**

German counter attacks

German 916 Infantry Regiment telephoned the 352nd Divisional Headquarters stating: 'weak enemy units had penetrated Pointe du Hoc. A platoon from the 9th Company 726th Regiment had been dispatched to counter attack.' By mid-day the Germans had recognized that they were up against two companies inside the battery position. The 726th Regiment now confidently deployed the Stossreserve from the III Battalion to restore the situation.

That afternoon a message was received at V Corps Headquarters via the Navy saying:

'Located Pointe du Hoe [sic] – mission accomplished – need ammunition and reinforcement – many casualties.'

Cursed with radio communication difficulties throughout the day, the now greatly depleted Ranger force received a relayed message from General Huebner via the *Satterlee*.The message said simply:

'No Reinforcements Available.'

By nightfall the situation was looking desperate. As Samuel Elliot Morison described in his official history of the United States Navy: 'Throughout the day *Satterlee*, *Barton* and *Thompson* gave the Rangers fire support'. But at 2100, Rudder was still in a critical

Colonel Rudder during the battle at Ponte du Hoc.

situation, with one third of his men killed or wounded, and ammunition running low. Then 23 men from A Company, 5th Rangers appeared. Thirteen hours earlier they had become separated in the chaos at Omaha Beach as the initial American penetration was made between Vierville and St. Laurent. Their commander, Lieutenant Charles H. Parker Jr., led his men inland to their designated assembly area. No one else arrived at the rendezvous. In the finest traditions of manoeuvre warfare he followed through with his orders and headed for the Pointe. After fighting two engagements and capturing some 20 Germans, Parker and his men finally arrived at the Pointe. The last of three German counter-attacks against his perimeter that night broke through, and he had to withdraw to the Pointe into a 200 metre deep defended area.

Next day, 7th June, the Colonel had fewer than a hundred men left

After the battle – two days of fighting and rubble of smashed casemates at the Pointe. Prisoners are being taken down to the beach for evacuation to England.

who were fit to fight, and very little food. Thompson, which had been firing on call from the Rangers since daybreak, was relieved by Harding at 0606. A whaleboat sent in to evacuate casualties was so damaged by grounding on the rocky beach in a heavy sea and current that it was unable to retract. Around noon, Admiral Bryant contributed both food and ammunition from Texas to keep the Rangers fighting.'

In the face of stiff defence from the Rangers and pressure from the airborne and seaborne forces on either flank, the Germans actually withdrew on the 7th June. They then formed a new defensive line along the River Aure, just to the South of the N13 with remnants from the 352nd and 716th division. These troops had been fortunate enough to survive the initial battle for the foreshore and the lodgment.

It was not until the following day that relief arrived from Omaha Beach, almost 48 hours behind schedule. Just before midday on 8th

June the 1st Battalion 116th RCT supported by the 5th Ranger Battalion, relieved Rudder on the position.

The relief force from the 1st Battalion had cleared along the road from Vierville using the D514 as the axis of attack. The battalion had employed a Sherman tank company to blast a way through to Rudder and the surviving men in their 200-metre deep perimeter. Off the coast destroyers had once again provided vital supporting fire to the troops ashore as the 116th advanced to relieve the Rangers. This had been a remarkable battle in which the close cooperation between naval and ground forces once again proved decisive.

Postscript

At 1130 on 8th June 1944 the Stars and Stripes were raised at the Pointe du Hoc. Rudder 's force had suffered 70 percent casualties, overrun a fortified garrison and then held off five German counter-attacks. Before being relieved, however, Rudder's depleted force would be bombed and shelled by both Allied aircraft and friendly ground units. Rudder had been injured twice during the battle. Apart from his leg injury, he had been wounded in the arm by concrete splinters blown off one of the bunkers by 'friendly' naval gunfire.

Rudder would subsequently be awarded the Distinguished Service Cross for his action at Pointe du Hoc and go on to command the 109th Infantry Regiment from 8th December 1944 until the end of the war. He would lead that Regiment throughout the Battle of the Bulge in Luxembourg. Under his leadership the 109th Regiment would cripple the German advance on the southern flank and prevent any significant advance. For this action his Regiment received a Presidential Citation.

Before leaving the Pointe du Hoc consider these words from an inscription on the colonnade of the American Military Cemetery above Omaha Beach:
THIS EMBATTLED SHORE PORTAL OF FREEDOM IS FOREVER HALLOWED BY IDEALS, THE VALOUR AND THE SACRIFICES OF OUR FELLOW COUNTRYMEN

CHAPTER FIVE

THE 29th DIVISION UNITS AT OMAHA BEACH
Tour B-1

Route by Car to Omaha Beach

From the N13 turn north **towards the coast on the D6** towards Port en Bessin. As you enter the town t**urn left at the crossroads** onto the **D514** and head west towards Colleville-sur-Mer and Grandcamp-Maisy. After 1 kilometre you will enter the village of **Huppain**. Stop on the outskirts of this village and look north and south; this line represents the boundary between the British Second Army and the United States First Army under General Omar N. Bradley. As you **drive out** of Huppain towards **Vierville-sur-Mer** consider the distance that you are travelling to the beach. The area between Huppain and Cabourg was the D-Day objective for the 3rd Battalion of the 16th Regiment (3/16 Bn). In reality they would not achieve this objective until after D-Day, when a link up would take place between the 1st Division and the British 47 Commando on 8th June at Port-en-Bessin.

As you enter the village of **Colleville-sur-Mer** note that this was a German resistance point holding up the 16th Infantry Regiment on D-Day. After leaving Colleville you will see signs to the American National Cemetery and memorial at St Laurent, **ignore** them for the time being and drive on towards Vierville-sur-Mer. As you **enter Vierville turn right** down the **D.517** into the 'Vierville Draw.' Approximately half way to the seafront you should park and note the memorial to the 29th Infantry Division ('The Blue

The Vierville Draw and D-1 Exit.

The National Guard memorial placed on the German 75mm gun casemate (WN72) at the junction of Dog Green and Charlie.

Looking west along Charlie Sector. Note the cliff path on the left.

The cliff path above Charlie Sector.

and the Gray') sited to the right of the road on the grassed area. From here go to the sea front and **park near the Hotel du Casino**.

Visit the German fortifications and use the **National Guard Memorial as an initial viewpoint**. Look left at the Pointe et Raz de la Percée which is the prominent outcrop 2000 meters away. Look right along the beach and displayed before you is the 7000-meter crescent of Omaha Beach. Note the typical dominating position of this well sited German bunker.

View from 75mm gun emplacement WN72 at exit D-1, Vierville, three months after the battle.

Omaha sector

Omaha sector is about 25 kilometres long from the mouth of the Vire River in the west to the western edge of Port-en-Bessin to your east. You are now standing on the boundary between Charlie Beach and Dog White Beach. One thousand meters to your east is the boundary with Dog White Beach (on a line with Hamel-au-Prêtre). Five further beach sectors, all sub-divisions of Omaha Beach, extend beyond Dog White.

Look back up the Vierville draw and note the German fortifications on the upper eastern cliff face. These are the remains of WN 68. Consider how easily defended, or blocked, this gully would be under the control of well-motivated and well-equipped troops. These gun positions were able to fire down onto the beach and interlock their arcs of fire with similar positions sited behind the Hotel. Similar outposts covered each beach exit, or draw as the Americans refer to them.

109

There are a total of five draws off the beach. The operations order for Omaha Beach identified this exit as D-1. Two thousand meters away to your right is the Les Moulins draw that was designated as exit D-3. A further 1200 meters beyond that is Exit E-1 which marks the base of the hill upon which the American National Cemetery and Monument is now located overlooking Easy Green and Easy Red sectors. Beyond that are Exits that lead up to Colleville, 1500 meters behind the beach.

Having established your bearings **walk a short distance along the cliff base path towards the West**. You will follow the narrow road past the fishing pier on your right and with the bungalows and houses on your left. You should soon see the German fortifications on the cliff face in front of you. **Use the cliff path beyond the houses** to climb up to the fortifications. Half way to the top of the cliffs you can stop for a rest at the conveniently sited stone bench in front of the first bunker. **Follow the path** up to the German emplacements at the top. From here you have a superb view of the coast and along the length of the beach. This will be **Stand 1**.

Stand 1: The Assault by 116th RCT, 29th Division, from Vierville and St. Laurent.

At 0625 hours the preplanned bombardment of coastal defences ceased after the ships had fired over 3,000 rounds at the specified targets ashore. British LCTs then fired their barrages of 5-inch rockets, many of them falling short of the defences. A short distance behind them, the remaining seagoing DD tanks from the 741st Tank Battalion supporting 1st Division were struggling to shore pursued by the infantry landing craft. In the 29th Division group the 743rd Tank Battalion with its 32 DD tanks had more success. A Navy

Landing craft closing in on Omaha Beach at around 6.30 am.

Lieutenant seeing the fate of the 741st decided to bring his LCTs into the beach and so gave the tankers a fighting chance. They would, however, be leaderless. The battalion commander's LCT was sunk off the beach, and all other officers except one lieutenant were killed or wounded. The tanks that landed opposite the Vierville draw from Company B fell easy pray to the German artillery and cannons sited to protect this beach exit, however eight of them did engage targets as soon as they landed. Tanks from A and C Companies would be more fortunate landing on Dog White and Red in good order.

The first infantry wave was organized in boat sections of six LCVPs or LCAs. Each section carried a company of assault troops with associated headquarters groups following-on at 0700 in the second wave. Each boat was organized in a similar manner with one officer and 31 troops distributed as follows:

One NCO and five riflemen in the bow
Wire cutting team: four men tasked to breach wire entanglements
Two Browning Automatic Rifle (BAR) teams of two men each
Two bazooka teams
Four-man mortar team with 60mm mortar
Flame-thrower team
Demolition team equipped with prepared TNT charges
Medic and section commander in the stern
Coxswain.

Each boat endured a similar journey to the beach. The men were quickly soaked by the cold drenching spray, many were uncontrollably sea sick and at least ten infantry carrying landing craft sank, having shipped too much water during the protracted

run-in. Each man was overloaded with his equipment and further discomforted in the cramped conditions. If a boat sank few men could survive in the water with 40-60 pounds of gear strapped to them. One LCA carrying men from Company A, 116th RCT, foundered about 1,000 yards offshore; forbidden to stop and help, Rangers in passing craft watched men being dragged down by their loads. In an interview Lieutenant James 'Jack' Carroll described his memories of this journey:

'People were throwing up all over the boat, trying to avoid each other. Some just stood there in silence. It took us a long time to cover the six miles from the release point to the beach, a long time.'

Initially some of the assault troops thought that it all appeared as if this was another rehearsal at Slapton Sands then they noticed small yellow life rafts in the water with a few men clinging to them. These were the handful of survivors from the 27 drowned DD tanks. Of their 135 crewmen few would survive. Others noted the approaching shoreline. At this point there was no sign of the Germans as Captain Sabin USN recalled:

'As we went towards the beach, there was no sign of life or resistance. Approaching closer, the concrete wall just to the East of Dog Green became plainly visible. There appeared to be openings along its length. Some structures which appeared to be pillboxes, a few houses, and the church steeple at Vierville were sighted. There was an intense quiet, so quiet it was suspicious.'

As the coastal bombardment had ceased the 600 to 800 German troops awaiting the V Corps rushed to their appointed defensive positions and prepared for battle. Weapons and ammunition were prepared, arcs of fire and vision slits cleared of debris, while commanders along the bluffs and in the resistance nests checked the range of the approaching fleet. Orders were clear – no firing until the landing craft beach at the water line. Shortly after 0630 hours the first boats amongst the 48 craft heading for the beach touched down. The carefully laid plans of the Allied generals, and the hopes and prayers of all the Allied soldiers and sailors were all dashed to naught in a few ghastly moments. Ted Lombarski was a sergeant in F Company, 16th RCT. He recalled:

'Can you picture the Germans waiting for us? They only had to fire on the LCVPs as we landed. There were so many bullets zeroing in on the first wave that it was impossible to cross the beach. Being in the first wave was like committing suicide. Yet some of us did cross the beach and reach the shale. Here we had protection from small-

Closing in when 'all-hell-let-loose' on Omaha.

arms fire. In front of the shale were mines, barbed wire, and the Germans raining bullets all over. All this plus mortars and anti-tank guns, and artillery – all zeroed in on the beach. If you exposed yourself you were dead. We were brave and we had a job to do, but we weren't stupid. If you exposed yourself you were a casualty, and dead soldiers don't help anyone.

I'll say it again: E and F Companies were on a suicide mission. It's a miracle any of us survived.'

Similar conditions were experienced by most of the initial wave. As we now know, the Germans had been left pretty much unscathed by the preparatory bombardment. Alert to the approaching threat, the veteran German troops in the 352nd were steadying the nerves of the weaker soldiers from the 716th Division. As the landing craft approached them in a frontal attack they could focus their well-planned defensive fires onto a limited number of targets. Each target craft presented its human cargo in a tightly confined space (the landing craft) with only one exit down the bow ramp. Wherever landing craft beached directly beneath German strongpoints, or one of the 85 supporting machine gun posts, the results were terrible for the men struggling through the surf to the shore. German machine gunners and artillery observers had plenty of time to track their targets into appointed

Ted Lombarski

113

When the initial bombadment ended 600 to 800 German troops awaiting V Corps rushed to their appointed defensive positions. They were able to radio that the invasion had begun.

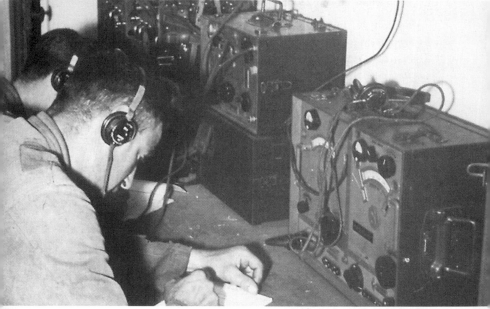

engagement areas. As the craft approached, one German observer from the 352nd Artillery Regiment reported:

> 'Something like 60 to 80 fast landing craft are approaching the coast near Colleville. These boats cannot be reached by our own artillery... the battleships in the foreground are too far away for our own artillery to reach.'

With an inevitability that must have been full of expectation, fear and grim reality, the two opposing forces drew closer together. At the appointed moment German commanders ordered their men to fire. Their targets were about a quarter of a mile from them. The silent shore now turned into hell. Sergeant Golas of the 2nd Ranger Battalion was approaching Charlie Beach below the cliffs west of Vierville when the fire began. He said to his friends in surprise 'Gee fellas they are shooting back at us!' Any hopes of an unopposed landing on a benign shore were gone. That dawning realization must have been appalling as the sound of impacting machine gun bullets striking the forward ramps of the landing craft reached the ears of the young men contained within them. Trapped but momentarily protected by their craft, the soldiers and Rangers knew that their protective shield would soon disappear and they would be naked to the impact of the scything, deadly fire now playing a murderous beat on the forward ramps. For these unfortunate men there was no place to hide. As William Cambell further along the beach with the 18th RCT headquarters stated afterwards: 'it was a pretty good killing zone in there... the fire was especially heavy on the beach.' Charles Hangsterfer also of the 1st Division remembers:

Charles Hangsterfer

> 'My friend Al Smith was in the same LCVP I was, and we could see that some of the LCVPs were hitting these mines and blowing up. And I'm shouting over the roar of the boat's engine, 'Open the ramp!' and he's shouting, 'keep the ramp up!'
>
> I didn't know why he gave that order. I didn't question it however. But on the 40th Anniversary of the landing, when we were touring Omaha Beach, I finally asked him, 'Why did you do that?' He told me that machine-gun bullets had been hitting the front of the ramp, and he was not about to let it down.'

Hangsterfer's boat team would be landed on Easy Red along with a confused mix of the 116th RCT from 29th Division. As Bill Friedman

Survivors struggled forward discarding equipment and seeking what limited shelter was available amongst the waves or behind the beach defences.

observed, this type of operation is chaos incarnate at the best of times, but Omaha was turning into something much worse.

Other assault boats would be less fortunate than Hangsterfer's men. Company A of the 29th Division suffered a terrible fate. During the run-in two out of the six company boats were lost. As the remainder approached the beach they ignored the machine-gun fire on the closed boat ramps and in the surf around them and faced their enemy head-on. They made the ultimate sacrifice for their courage. LCA1015 carrying 32 'Stonewallers' from 116th RCT of the 29th Division was completely annihilated; the men were riddled in their craft and as they exited, including the company commander, Captain Taylor Fellers. He had taken his men all the way to the correct objective only to be slaughtered. Along Dog Green beach just to the East of the mouth of the Vierville draw the three other remaining first wave craft from Company A were also hit by concentrated fire. The National Guard Memorial in front of the Hotel Du Casino now overlooks their landing site.

At 0638 hours the USS *McCook* action report stated:

'First landing craft containing men and material made landing on beach. Enemy fire severe from unknown points.'

As the men from Company A left their craft they were cut down by that fire on their boat ramps, falling headlong, dead or wounded into the frigid water. Men further to the rear in the boats leapt over the sides in an effort to avoid the deadly fire. For them another fate awaited as they plunged into deeper water, overloaded with packs and weapons. Many would drown. The horrified survivors and the wounded struggled forward discarding equipment and seeking what limited shelter was available amongst the waves or behind the beach defences. Those who tried to rush forward were cut-down as the Germans now sought to complete their deadly task.

While the infantry and surviving armour were trying to make the sea wall the Special Engineer Task Force consisting of Naval Combat

Out of the frying pan and into the fire – survivors from a sunken landing craft struggle onto the beach at Omaha and into a hail of bullets.

Demolitions Units and the 146th and 299th Battalions of Army Engineers were attempting to clear their designated 50-metre wide gaps in the beach obstacles. Working in the open without any cover other than the obstacles themselves, the Task Force was quickly decimated. The U.S. Army's official account stated 'casualties... ran to 41 percent for D-Day, most of them in the first half-hour'. When the follow-up waves landed on the rising tide most of the lethal obstacles would still be in place. Instead of clearing eight 50-metre gaps the 146th had blown only two small gaps in the 29th Division's sector. Six complete and three partial gaps would be made in total on Omaha but at a terrible cost. Even the supporting bulldozers were quickly reduced to three working vehicles on the beach. Ten had been lost on the run-in and three hit by gunfire as they manoeuvred across the beach.

Many engineers had been killed as German small-arms fire or direct hits from mortar and artillery rounds initiated their demolition packs. One naval team of 8 men was blown to pieces when their pre-loaded rubber boat was hit by shrapnel from a bursting shell, only one of the men survived. Others had been prevented from blowing obstacles because desperate survivors from the first wave were hiding beneath them. Another team had successfully prepared a 30-metre gap for blowing when a mortar round set off their prima cord. Nineteen engineers and infantrymen were killed or wounded in that conflagration. As with the assault companies, many engineer craft had been swept to the East further compounding the situation between Charlie and Easy Green (beyond the Les Moulins draw). One LCM received a direct hit as the demolition team approached the beach. The explosives on deck were detonated killing the entire navy team. Even individual engineers were blown to pieces as their explosive charges were struck by bullets and shell fragments as they crossed the beach.

After the battle the 116th Regiment prepared a report from the accounts of the survivors of the first wave. General Gerhardt later authorized the report. This extract provided by Private (Pte) Howard L. Gresser, captures with horrific clarity the experiences of the men caught on the beach at the moment they landed:

'As if this had been the signal for which the enemy waited, the ramps were instantly enveloped in a crossing of automatic fire which was accurate and in great volume. It came at the boats from both ends of the beach. Company 'A' had planned to move in three files from each boat, centre file going first, then flank files peeling off to

lhe right and left. The first men tried it. They crumpled as they sprang from the ship, forward into the water. Then order was lost. It seemed to the men that the only way to get ashore with a chance of safety was to dive head first into the water.'

The report continued, telling the story of the men as they struggled to shore. Private First Class (Pfc.) Gilbert G. Murdock remembered that:

'Many were lost before they had a chance to face the enemy. Some of them were hit in the water and wounded. Some drowned then. Others, wounded, dragged themselves ashore and upon finding the sand lay quiet and gave themselves shots, only to be caught and drowned within a few minutes by the on-racing tide.'

Murdock went on to describe how others successfully crossed the fire swept surf and reached the beach only to return to the water to find some cover. He recalled 'Many were shot while doing so. Those who survived kept moving shoreward with the tide and in this way finally made their landing.' Private First Class (Pfc.) Leo J. Nash described the state of Company A as 'inert, leaderless and almost incapable of action.' Most of the young officers were dead within minutes of landing. Nash observed Lieutenant Edward Tidrick being hit in the throat as he leapt from the boat ramp. He got to the

The German defenders were able to put up a withering fire from their *Wiederstandsnest* (restistance points) which consisted of concrete gun emplacements and support trenches. Here Atlantic Wall garrison troops man their positions prior to D-Day.

beach and 'flopped down' wounded before raising himself up again to give Nash an order: 'Advance with the wire cutters!' At that moment Nash watched in horror as the officer was cleaved by machine gun fire from head to pelvis. Another boat came in close by containing men from a medical section; they too were cut down by German fire.

Within 15 to 20 minutes Company A was a shattered force having lost over 60 percent of its men. The remaining group of survivors would be incapable of conducting effective operations until reconstituted over the next few days. The unscathed survivors now set about finding cover from the German fire and staying alive. Some discarded all their equipment and helped pull their wounded comrades out of the rising water and onto the beach. Again, many of these rescuers were caught by German fire.

Immediately to the West of the Vierville draw Company C of the 2nd Rangers landed as planned on Charlie beach but within the arcs of fire of the cliff top and beach front strongpoints. They suffered a similar fate to Company A and within minutes half the force was dead or wounded. They would be incapable of completing their mission on D-Day which had been to gain the cliff top and advance West to the Pointe de la Percée and destroy a German strongpoint that could fire onto Omaha Beach. The destroyers offshore would complete this task. At 0716 hours the USS *Thompson* logged:

'Field gun observed firing on beachhead from approximately 636982 [Pointe de la Percée]. Commenced firing... 0755 Ceased fire on the above target. Target destroyed.'

Amidst this chaos and carnage on the beach came Company B in their landing craft at 0700 hours and Company D ten minutes later. Both of these sub-units beached on Charlie and Dog Green at the mouth of the Vierville draw. Though dispersed, they landed where they were supposed. Unfortunately they were also quickly decimated by the well-sited and as yet undisrupted German strongpoints dominating the foreshore.

While this slaughter was taking place on Dog Green one unforeseen effect of the poor preliminary bombardment was having positive results further to the East. The grass on the bluffs to the West of the D-3 exit had caught fire and the billowing smoke was obscuring the Germans' view of Dog Red and to a lesser extent Dog White an area from Hamel-au-Prêtre to the Les Moulins draw. The companies approaching these beaches would be fortunate. Six boats from Company G had drifted left and beached just West of Les

Moulins. Concealed by the smoke from the effects of accurate German defensive fire the Stonewallers lumbered across 350 metres of open sand in good order to the seawall. Here commanders realized that the men were misplaced and instead of moving forward up the bluffs an order was passed along the line to 'Move to the right 1,000 yards. You are to the left of your target.' As this wasteful adjustment was made the soldiers began to take casualties along the beach front, a few seeing what was happening sought shelter while others decided to move to the bluffs.

Company F was also to benefit from the smoke obscuration. Landing to the right of Company G and just West of the Les Moulins draw they were actually in the cone of fire from WN 66 and 67 on the bluffs above and the strongpoints at the mouth of the draw. The smoke concealed them enough to avoid the fate of Company A 2,000 metres to their right. Some sections crossed the open beach in good order, while others were caught by German fire and sought shelter amongst the beach obstacles. Private John Robertson was lying at the water's edge when he saw a Sherman tank coming through the surf towards him. He recalled 'crossing the beach looked like suicide, but better than getting run over'. He sprinted to the cover of the sea wall.

The most chaotic landing was made by Company E. This company had been ordered to land at the eastern end of the 29th Division 's sector but the impact of tide, obscuration of identifiable features, fear, and the confusion of battle, scattered the boats over a 1,000 metre frontage amongst the 1st Division. Most of these boats beached over a mile from Les Moulins leaving the company commander with the difficult task of establishing some form of order and a link to the rest of the distant battalion. The fate of the company was mixed. Two boats made perfect landings in a lightly defended area. Only two men were hit as the troops rushed the 300 metres to the seawall. The remaining four boats were less fortunate with one craft being hit by artillery fire and the other boat sections being caught by the hail of small arms fire sweeping and plunging onto the beach. The company commander, Captain Lawrence Madill encouraged his men forward. Walter E. Smith of Company E saw him:

> 'Captain Madill came up behind me and others, ordering all that could move to get off the beach. I looked up at him and his left arm appeared to be almost blown off.'

Even in this agonized state Madill led by example. Seeing one of his mortars being set up, he ran out into the surf to recover its ammunition. As he approached the mortar team he was cut down by machine gun fire and gasped his last order: 'Senior non-com, take the men off the beach'.

By 0700 hours it was clear to those on the beach that the first wave from the 116th RCT and the Rangers had failed to achieve their mission. Within half an hour of landing Company A from the 116th, Company C from the 2nd Rangers and the engineers were shattered having been cut to pieces on the open beach or in their boats. Company E was lost and disorientated and now landing with the 1st Division to the East, while Companies G and F were scattered, disorganized and suffering heavy casualties as the troops tried to get to their objectives or simply awaited their fate in the surf or behind the sea wall. As a result the scene that greeted the next waves were anything but planned.

By 0700 hours the rising tide had reached the rows of obstacles and within the hour the water would be up a further 8 feet covering the obstacles and drowning the weak and wounded too incapacitated to move further up the beach. The German defences were still effective and no advance had been made beyond the shingle embankment or the sea wall. Still debilitated by the hours of seasickness endured during the run-in, now leaderless, cold and wet with many men in shock at the carnage around them, the remnants of the first wave could do little more than try to survive until the follow-on companies brought reinforcements and hope. Meanwhile, some astute infantrymen set about cleaning their weapons for the fight ahead while others tended to, or rescued, the wounded in the surf. The dead were left to roll in to the beach amongst the waves and the flotsam and jetsam of battle.

At 0641 hours aboard the USS *Ancon* the 1st Division's G-3 duty officer entered into his Operations Journal a report received from Patrol Craft 552 to the *Ancon*. It said tersely: 'entire first wave foundered.'

Before leaving Stand 1 let us consider the fate of the Provisional Ranger Force and the infantry companies landing from 0700-0730 hours in front of Vierville draw and the Les Moulins draw 2,000 metres to your East. Because of the early mishaps delaying Rudder's escalade attack on the Pointe du Hoc , the eight 65 man companies of the Provisional Ranger Force waiting offshore for his success signal were redirected to their alternative landing site – Vierville. Colonel Max Schneider had assumed that Rudder had failed and

Major General Charles Gerhardt and his staff observe the initial assault wave floundering in the surf. Their concern is evident.

now his elite force was on the way towards 'Bloody Omaha.' Their secondary mission was to beach behind the 116th and move overland as quickly as possible to Pointe du Hoc – avoiding all unnecessary contact. Speed was of the essence. At the Pointe they were to link up with the survivors of Rudder's force, complete the destruction of the gun battery and then move inland to cut the Grandcamp-Vierville road.

With the majority of Schneider's force landing behind Company C of the 116th in a weakly defended sector the Rangers made a successful crossing of the beach. Two other companies that had landed on target at Vierville were caught in the same killing area that had reduced Company A of the 116th to a shattered group of desperate survivors. Quickly reduced to half strength even this elite group could do little other than shelter at the top of the beach amongst the debris of Company A.

The rest of Schneider's force now set about taking the fight to the enemy. They would play a major role as the morning wore on, in penetrating the defences astride the Les Moulins draw and sweeping around to Vierville in an attempt to get to Pointe du Hoc.

The other companies from the 116th RCT landed as follows:

Company B (1st Battalion, 116th RCT) landed at 0700 hours on Charlie beach just West of the Vierville draw. There they were decimated and the company commander Captain Ettore Zappacosta cut down ten yards from his boat screaming 'I'm hit' before disappearing beneath the waves. Every man except one was killed or wounded from that boat.

Company C (1st Battalion, 116th RCT) landed at 0710 hours on Dog Green midway between Vierville and Hamel au Prêtre. Under cover of smoke they made it across the beach with minimal losses.

Company D (1st Battalion, 116th RCT) landed at 0710 hours on Dog Green just to the East of the draw. The company commander, Captain Walter Schilling was killed when his boat struck a mine. He was now the fourth company commander to die that morning. Three of those company commanders were from the 1st Battalion alone. Other Company D boats had similar fates. Sergeant William Norfleet had to force his British Coxswain to take his craft further inshore because the water was too deep where he had stopped. As they closed on the beach it too hit an obstacle and sank but the men made it in through the waist deep water.

Company H (2nd Battalion, 116th RCT) landed at 0700 hours on the boundary between Dog White and Dog Red 480 yards West of Les Moulins. There the 'Twentyniners' were opposite WN 66 and 67 and again these men paid a heavy price on the beach. In one instance a Private recalled watching two of his buddies seeking shelter behind a Tetrahedron only to see it driven back into them by a bursting artillery shell. He recalled: 'I tried to peel the steel loose from the men, but couldn't do it. Then I figured they were dead anyway.' Major Bingham, commanding the 2nd Battalion had landed slightly East of Company H. He remembered:

'I thought all was well until, after struggling ashore through shoulder-deep water, I paused for a breather behind a steel tetrahedron anti-boat obstacle and noticed the sand kicking up at my feet... I was getting shot at... From then on, there was no doubt in my mind. I was scared, exhausted... I finally crossed the beach and got to the shingle along the beach road where about 100 men from Company F were seeking what little shelter the road afforded.'

124

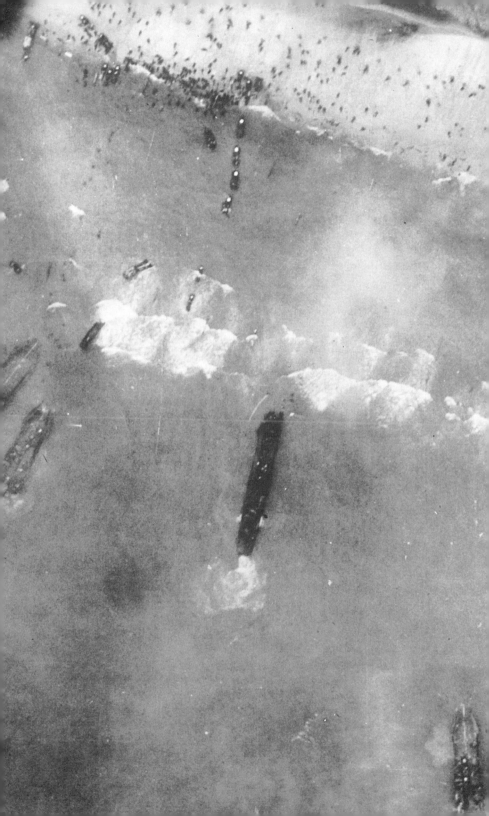

Companies I and K (3rd Battalion, 116th RCT) landed at 0720 hours on Easy Green and just East of the D-3 or Les Moulins draw. They actually landed relatively intact. In Company K the only known casualty before the troops reached the seawall was a Lieutenant accidentally stabbed by a bayonet while still aboard his LCVP.

Companies L and M (3rd Battalion, 116th RCT) landed between 0720 and 0727 hours over 600 yards East of Les Moulins on the 1st Divisions designated beaches. These men also fared well in comparison to the hapless companies of the 1st Battalion. One Company M Sergeant stated, 'The Company learned with surprise how much small arms fire a man can run through without getting hit.' However, many of these men were debilitated by the effects of being in their cramped boats for several hours.

Into the chaos on Dog White at 0730 hours came General Cota aboard LCVP 71 accompanying Colonel Canham and his staff from the 116th. By chance they had come in at a decisive point along the foreshore. Concealed by the smoke from the burning grass on the bluffs, they landed in relatively good order. Around them they found Company C and a mixture of Rangers and 2nd Battalion men seeking cover. Behind them were the approaching landing craft bringing the 5th Ranger Battalion's companies ashore. Unfortunately disaster struck the 116th Regiment's backup headquarters aboard LCI(L)-91. This craft was hit by artillery fire and exploded in flames killing everyone in the forward compartment. A similar fate awaited LCI(L)-92 beaching five minutes later in the same area. An underwater obstacle had exploded, igniting the craft's fuel tanks. These two LCIs were to burn for much of the day.

Brigadier General Cota and Colonel Canham were about to play a major role in getting the 29th Division off the beach and up the bluffs. That movement forward would start in the area between the D-1 and D-3 draws from about 0750 hours onwards and be executed by Company C led by a few exceptionally brave 'Twentyniners.' Small groups ranging from a dozen troops to a weak company of 100 men had rationalized that it would be safer to fight their way off the beach than remain in this rapidly deteriorating killing area. Further to the East along the beach Colonel Taylor of the 16th RCT would reach the same conclusion and galvanize his veteran regiment with a legendary speech: 'Two kinds of people are staying on this beach, the dead and those who are going to die. Now lets get the hell out of here'. That story will be told in more detail later.

While the situation was grim for the men pinned down on the beach there were rays of hope. From 0810 hours the destroyers of DESRON 18 began to break the cease fire order that had suspended naval gunfire support at 0630 hours. The USS *Carmick* was soon in action, responding to Shore Fire Control Party (SFCP) fire missions. The destroyer gunnery officer also demonstrated exemplary initiative as this action report entry from *Carmick* demonstrates:

'Early in the morning a group of tanks were seen to be having difficulty making their way along the breakwater road toward Exit D-1 [Vierville]. A silent cooperation was established wherein they fired at a target on the bluff above them and we then fired several salvoes at the same spot. They then fire further along the bluff and we used their bursts again as a point of aim. This continued as they slowly advanced along the breakwater.'

This timely cooperation proved essential in neutralizing or destroying some of the German positions formerly preventing movement towards the bluffs. By 0900 hours approximately 5,000 men had been landed on the beach.

To the army and naval commanders offshore it was clear that the landing was not going according to plan. Radio communications with the beach were at best sporadic. This added to the 'fog' surrounding events ashore. In the 116th RCT, for example, over three-quarters of the radios had already been lost. General Bradley now feared 'that our forces had suffered an irreversible catastrophe.' At 0900 hours when the pendulum of battle appeared to be slipping away from the Americans, Captain Sanders, commander of DESRON 18 in USS *Frankford*, ordered his destroyers to close on the beach and support the assault troops. At 0950 hours this was reinforced by a tactical voice radio message from Rear Admiral Carleton F. Bryant in *Texas*, to the commander of the Omaha bombardment force. It was sent in his clear voice for all to hear, it read:

'Get on them men, get on them. We must knock out those guns. They are raising hell with the men on the beach, and we can't have any more of that. We must stop it.'

The contribution made by the ships in the line was dramatic. General Gerow's first message from ashore to Bradley at the end of the day was an emotional acknowledgement of the navy's role in getting the men off the beach: 'Thank God for the U.S. Navy.'

It is remarkable to now piece the jig-saw of events together and

View along Omaha Beach looking towards the west.

realize that at 0900 hours movement up the bluffs had started in sufficient strength to threaten the cohesion of the German linear defences above the beach. In the West, elements of the Rangers and Company C, 116th were inland at Dog Green, while elements of Companies K, I and L of the 116th were also above the bluffs at Easy Green. In the East, troops from the 16th RCT were on the ridge between E-1 and E-3 behind Easy Red. At the F-1 draw – now beyond the American Cemetrey – Company L was preparing an assault up the steep draw towards Cabourg.

One hour later and in the absence of clear reports, General Bradley ordered Major Chester Hansen to the beach in a landing craft to gain a first hand situation report. From the *Augusta* to the beach was over 11 miles. At 1130 hours Hansen returned to the *Augusta* and reported 'Disaster lies ahead.' He had been unable to detect movement up the bluffs and reported the evident chaos and losses on the beach. Bradley, now disconnected from the battlefield and in the absence of accurate information, considered withdrawing the force and re-landing V Corps in the British sector. Worse still, and as a result of Bradley's inaccurate assessment reports back to SHAEF, Eisenhower issued an order to the Allied air forces to bomb Omaha Beach at 1330 hours. Fortunately, this proved impossible to achieve. It would have been an appalling and costly error of judgement.

The German Defenders Assessment

The 916th Regiment's troops opposing the 116th RCT had done well. They had absorbed the assault by the first wave and destroyed landing craft, tanks and American units in the well-planned killing areas along the shore. The commander of WN76 at the Pointe et Raz de la Percée (between Pointe du Hoc and Charlie sector where you are now) could observe the destruction of the first wave and the ensuing chaos amongst the follow-up craft as they negotiated the tide covered beach obstacles. Oberst (Colonel) Fritz Ziegelman, the '1A' or Chief of Staff of the 352nd Division went forward to the WN 76 command post during the early morning. A journey of 30 minutes had taken 5 hours because of enemy fighter patrols overhead. When he reached the cliff top command post Ziegelman was shocked by the view. He wrote later:

'The view will remain in my memory forever, the sea was like a picture of the Kiel review of the fleet.' Ships of all sorts stood close together on the beach and in the water, broadly echeloned in depth. And the entire conglomeration remained there intact without any real interference from the German side! I clearly understood the mood of the German soldier, who missed the Luftwaffe. It is a wonder that German soldiers fought hard and stubbornly here. '

Ziegelman was an experienced officer, he recognized the overwhelming force displayed before him. The only chance the 352nd Division had was to immediately snuff out any penetrations inland from the beach using local reserves. Other German soldiers briefly assumed that they had blunted the attack. The commander of WN76 reported to the 352nd Divisional headquarters:

'The enemy is in search of cover behind the coastal obstacles. A great many vehicles – among these ten tanks – stand burning on the beach. The obstacle demolition squads have given up their activity. Debarkation from the landing boats has ceased, the boats keep farther seawards. The fire of our strongpoints and artillery was well placed and has inflicted considerable casualties among the enemy. A great many wounded and dead lie on the beach.'

This kind of report during the early morning may have convinced General Kraiss that the evolving situation at Omaha was less of a threat than conditions further East. Initially he was right. Just after 0800 hours the divisional headquarters received a chilling message that 'something like 35 tanks are attacking over WN35 and 36 towards Arromanches'. This was a significant breakthrough by the British. As a result, Kraiss released two battalions from his divisional reserve to stem the penetration by the British 50th Division moving inland from Gold Beach, 15 miles East of the Omaha sector. Had those tactical reserves intervened in strength at Omaha Beach that afternoon, then the results could have been catastrophic for V Corps and for the overall cohesion of the Allied beachhead. This would have been particularly dangerous if the Germans had produced additional forces at Omaha when Bradley was already imagining the worst.

It is important at this point to remind oneself that the localized events at Omaha Beach were part of a much broader canvas. The chaotic drop of American airborne forces during the night of 6th June was now having a positive influence on the survival of the

Some German soldiers briefly assumed that they had blunted the attack at Omaha. They had responded effectively to the invaders – but V Corps men were determined to win through.

Omaha beachhead. Between 0200 and 0310 hours General Kraiss had assessed the reports of airborne landings along the boundary between the 352nd and the 709th Division as an attempt to cut him off from his western neighbour. So at 0310 hours he ordered *Kampfgruppe* (KG) Meyer (named after its commander Oberstleutnant Meyer) to deploy from its base near Bayeux to the Vire estuary to destroy this threat to his flank. KG Meyer consisted of so-called mobile infantry battalions. Their mobility was achieved by deploying the infantry on bicycles and the heavier weapons in a few motorized vehicles.

Yet KG Meyer was not only the 352nd Division's reserve it was also the 84th Corps, reserve on call to General Erich Marcks in Caen. Once mobile it was hard to control this key force because of a shortage of combat radios inherent amongst coastal defence and reserve units. At 0550 hours Kraiss realized that he had made a mistake in deploying over a third of his infantry strength against what were now clearly dispersed paratroopers. By this time a far greater threat was being reported by his coastal units. Kraiss now halted the eastward move of KG Meyer. It now sat immobile for two hours. At 0735 hours Kraiss ordered a single battalion (II/915th) to attack into the gap between WN 60 and 62 at the eastern end of Omaha Beach. This new threat had been reported to his headquarters from about 0720 hours onwards, as this divisional log book entry reveals:

'0725: One company is attacking in front of WN 60 and 62. Four further boats have landed in front of WN 61. One boat has been shot in flames by the 50mm gun. The enemy has penetrated WN 62 and at the same time WN 61 is being attacked from the beach in front and in the rear. Telephone connection with 1st Battalion 716th Regiment in Port-en-Bessin has been destroyed.'

The reserve battalion was expected to arrive in the area of Ste. Honorine-des-Pertes by 0930 hours. What was planned and what was in reality possible now proved very different. In the early morning light, Allied fighter-bombers were now active and interdicting all German road movement. The reserve would not reach the eastern beach area until mid afternoon, having been under constant air attack throughout the day. By that time the 3rd Battalion of the 16th RCT had made a decisive penetration to the outskirts of Ste Honorine.

To compound his problems, Kraiss would divide his reserve and send two other battalions towards the 50th Division's penetration inland from Gold Beach, North of Bayeux. Arriving late in the day and also severely battered by Allied fighters, this reserve was almost annihilated as it threw itself against the best part of a British division. By 2300 hours Meyer had been reported severely wounded and missing, presumed captured. His force had been reduced to two isolated groups, one of which was encircled at Bazenville 9 kilometres East of Bayeux, each numbering no more than 50 men supported by six surviving assault guns.

These events are significant to the study of the battle at Omaha Beach. They illustrate the chaotic conditions that tend to exist in any battle. That chaos has usually impeded the decision-making and actions of both opposing forces. To compound his problems Kraiss, rather like Bradley on USS *Augusta*, had been lacking effective, accurate and timely intelligence throughout D-Day. As a result he had been unaware of the mid-morning penetration by Cota's force to Vierville until as late as 1600 hours that day. So while things were looking grim on the beach for V Corps the Germans were also in a very bad way.

The tactical situation was confused and unclear even to local German commanders as communications systems collapsed or forward locations were overrun. Montgomery had been right to insist on the expansion of the COSSAC plan into the final, broader invasion front. That breadth of assault coupled with the use of airborne forces, decoys, deceptions and air-interdiction operations created sufficient confusion and friction to allow V Corps to get ashore and secure a beachhead without the intervention of a local German reserve.

All these different factors impacted on the Germans ability to use what limited reserves were available at the decisive point. With hindsight, it appears that Rommel had been right. The armoured reserves were needed well forward near the coast. They should also have been placed under a clear, well-informed, unified chain of command. Fortunately for the men pinned down on the beach at Vierville that did not exist in OB West on 6th June 1944.

The Penetration up the Bluffs by 29th Division

The initial wave from the 29th Division had lost 75 per cent of its radios and a high proportion of its junior leaders. If it was to get off the beach it now needed to have that missing leadership reimposed. Brigadier General Cota and Colonel Charles D. W. Canham of 116th

RCT had quickly realized this and set about taking command of the troops around them. Identifying areas of weaker German resistance they commenced breaching the obstacles along the promenade and leading their men off the beach. Cota's story is a remarkable example of senior leadership and intervention in battle at the critical moment both in time and space. The pendulum of battle was about to swing in the 29th Division's favour.

Initially, Cota identified a suitable location behind some cover for a BAR man to set up his gun and engage the German positions on the bluffs above. Under covering fire another brave 'Twentyniner' then went forward on Cota's orders to the barbed wire obstacle and blew a gap using a bangalore torpedo (a long tube packed with explosive designed to blow apart and cut through wire obstacles). The first man through the gap was cut down by German fire sobbing 'Mama' before dying where he fell. Cota realized that unless he did something no one would go through the wire. He rushed for the gap and went through the wire and across the road. Fortunately he made it and shouted to his men to follow him. They rushed for the gap. Remarkably no one was hit and he found himself directing this motley group through the 100 yards of tall grass and reeds beyond the road to the base of the bluffs. An empty German communications trench provided additional cover as they moved slowly forward. Once out of the trench they were in a minefield and several men were severely wounded by anti-personnel mines. From the upper slope they could look back at the beach where they witnessed an act of complete savagery. They saw five German prisoners being escorted to the beach by a 'Twentyniner'. The group came under fire from a German gun and two men fell dead. Lieutenant Jack Shea (Cota's aide) now recounts the story:

'Their captor dove towards the protecting cover of the seawall, while two of the remaining three sank to their knees... They seemed to be pleading with the operator of the machine gun, situated on the bluffs to the East, not to shoot them. The next burst caught the first kneeling German full in the chest, and as he crumpled the remaining two took to the cover of the seawall with their captor.'

At 0900 hours, two and a half-hours after the initial wave had started to land, Cota's group reached the top of the bluffs. The General then organized his men into fire teams and directed them forward to successfully attack an individual German machine gun before reaching a track running from the Les Moulins draw to

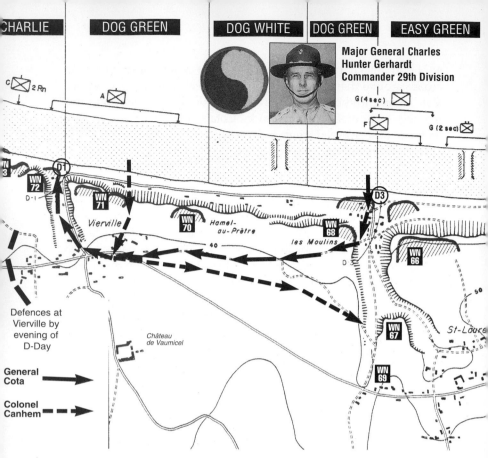

CHARLIE | DOG GREEN | DOG WHITE | DOG GREEN | EASY GREEN

Major General Charles
Hunter Gerhardt
Commander 29th Division

Defences at
Vierville by
evening of
D-Day

Château
de Vaumicel

General
Cota

Colonel
Canhem

Vierville. Turning right, they advanced to Vierville and met their
first terrified French citizens. At the outskirts of the village further
members of the 116th joined them, mostly from Company C. These
men recalled meeting Cota who was walking calmly down the main
street twirling his pistol. He greeted them with 'Where the hell have
you been boys?' Canham was also approaching Vierville with his
group. On arrival he deployed his men in a loose perimeter around
the south and west of the village. After linking up and conferring,
these two remarkable leaders now agreed to take a draw each.
Canham would go east and unplug the Les Moulins draw, attacking
the German defences from the rear, while Cota would move down
the Vierville draw and clear the remaining German positions that
were now coming under accurate naval gunfire.

With only five other men, Cota walked down the draw. By the
time they reached the mouth towards the beach the naval
bombardment by *Texas* (firing six 14-inch shells into the German

strongpoint between 1223 and 1230 hours) and the destroyers had ceased. After a brief firefight, five dazed Germans emerged from the fortifications to surrender to this ridiculously weak conquering force. Using the Germans as guides Cota then crossed a minefield and reached the beach where an appalling scene of destruction and carnage greeted him. The beach was covered with dead, many of them clearly identifiable from their blue and gray shoulder patches as 'Twentyniners'.

Having already cleared the Vierville draw from the rear, Cota was galvanized into further action. He set about pushing the infantry up the draw, while organizing the surviving engineers to blow the concrete anti-tank barrier that was still preventing vehicles and armour from advancing up the re-entrant. By midnight on 6th June the Vierville draw would be secure. The coast road would be cut and elements of the 1st and 2nd Battalions of the 116th would have established a necklace of positions to the South and West of the village. Between these two units were the 2nd and 5th Ranger Battalions now fixed for the night by stubborn German outposts separating them from their comrades under siege at the Pointe du Hoc .

After his very personal intervention at Vierville and after freeing the men on the beach from their inaction, Cota now moved east along the beach encouraging the rest of the men forward. Further along the beach and beyond the Les Moulins draw, another group from Company L, and G was being led forward by Lieutenant Donald Anderson. At the top of the bluffs he was shot through the jaw while trying to identify the location of a German machine gun post. With Anderson lying wounded a sergeant immediately took over and destroyed the gun position. Anderson survived the battle and was subsequently awarded a Silver Star for his leadership and courage. His group pressed on.

Around midday on the 6th June, the 3rd Battalion of the 116th RCT along with elements from the 2nd Battalion had reached the forward German defences at St. Laurent that were still plugging the exit from the Les Moulins draw. Repeated attempts to clear the positions failed and caused more casualties to Company L than had been suffered during their initial crossing of the beach. They were soon to be reinforced by the 115th RCT.

Colonel Eugene N. Slappey commanded the 115th RCT that had been designated as the V Corps floating reserve. It was off the beach in twelve LCIs, each fitted with two forward landing ramps for the

230 men aboard. Aboard the *Ancon*, General Gerow realized that the first wave was in severe difficulties so he authorized the landing of both the 1st and 29th Division's reserves. At 0930 hours the 18th Infantry had started to land in support of the 16th RCT at the eastern end of the beach. At about 1030 hours the 115th were approaching the beach to support the beleaguered 116th RCT. Slappey had planned to land at the Les Moulins draw but the destruction, obstacles and beached and burning craft from the first wave prevented that. The LCIs swung East and came in behind the 18th RCT in the 1st Divisions landing area at Easy Red , adding to the congestion and chaos. Once ashore Slappey met up with the 1st Division's assistant divisional commander, Brigadier General Willard Wyman. The two commanders now improvised a new plan to clear the village of St. Laurent held by a German company of infantry that was dominating the exits from the D-3 and E-1 draws.

Slappey was to get his three battalions off the beach and attack the village using the 1st Battalion as a fixing force, cutting the village off from reinforcement from the South while also covering exits from the village into the hinterland. Meanwhile his other two battalions were to mount an assault from the East.

The 115th moved very slowly off the beach. As Sergeant Charles Zarfass of Company A recalled: 'We moved cautiously and hesitantly, partly because of the strangeness of the situation.' The fear of mines and the continued sniping and incoming artillery fire also slowed their advance to a crawl. It would be late in the afternoon before the 2nd Battalion launched its attack and 1800 hours before the 1st Battalion reached its cut off position south of the village. The German garrison fought resolutely and in fact the village of St. Laurent would not fall until 7th June.

For their first three days in combat the 115th would be awarded 28 Distinguished Service Crosses and the Distinguished Unit Citation. But what had been happening to the 1st Division?

The heavy price of success at 'Bloody Omaha'.

CHAPTER SIX

ASSAULT BY THE 1st DIVISION
Tour B-2

Stand 2: E-1 Draw via the Junction of Dog and Easy Sectors, and the Village of St. Laurent

Descend from the cliff top back to the National Guard Monument. Note the fisherman's pier to your left. It was made after the war as an extension to a beached section of the Mulberry Harbour destroyed by the great Channel storm of June 1944. Walk out onto the pier to get a landing craft view of the bluffs and the fortified draw. Rejoin your vehicle and **drive along the promenade** stopping at appropriate points of interest on your way to the next stand.

Drive east noting the other beached concrete element of the Mulberry. On your right across the road you will see a memorial marker to the first American military cemetery sited here before the dead were re-interred and centralized at St. Laurent. As you approach the **junction where the D517 turns** inland and up through the Les Moulins draw, please note the memorial stone inlaid in the seawall on you left commemorating Operation Aquatint of 12th September 1942. This British commando raid was a disaster with its commander, Major March-Phillips drowning and two others being shot by the Germans on 13th September. They are now buried in the St. Laurent-sur-Mer village cemetery. Continue to the Comité du Debarquement memorial with its side panels to the 116th RCT 29th Division and the 1st Division. This sits at the junction between Dog and Easy sectors.

German 50mm gun position WN72 – looking West.

German strong point WN64 with its 50 mm gun still in place. Inside the bunker the damage to the gun can be examined along with the scoring on the concrete where 37mm shells and .5 calibre machine gun bullets entered the embrasure. Two half-tracks belonging to 467th Anti-Aircraft Artillery Battalion engaged the gun from the water's edge – the combined fire power of six machine guns and the cannon sufficed to wreck the German gun. It is not known if the crew survived the concentrated fire. The damage to the roof was caused by a naval shell shortly after the position had been neutralized.

WN64 with its support trenches was captured by Company E, 16th Infantry. Forty German defenders were killed in the action to take this position. After its capture the engineers took over the 50mm casemate as their headquarters.

Select a place to stop and examine the dominant bluffs, the open ground from the shingle embankment (marked by the new sea wall) to the base of the bluffs and the Les Moulins draw.

Now **drive up the D517** to the village of **St. Laurent** and identify a small **left hand turn** that will take you East down to the E-1 Exit. The minor road is located **250 metres North of the D514**. Park your vehicle in the village and walk down the minor road to E-1.As the narrow road turns North to the sea and descends down the western side of the wooded valley note the terrain as you see it from the German defenders perspective. As you walk along the road note the forward spur on your left. On the crest at the end of the spur was the site of General Gerow's V Corps headquarters. It was established ashore after 2000 hours on 6th June. Also note on your right that the forward, lower end of the spur across the valley was the site of German strongpoint WN 64. Above that spur on the crest you will be able to see the American Cemetery at St. Laurent.

As you reach the end of the spur you will see part of WN 65 on your left. The remaining blockhouse was at the centre of the strongpoint and was classed as a Type 667 Casemate equipped with a 50-mm gun. Note the design of the blockhouse and its oblique view of the beach. The protective wall facing the sea made the muzzle flash hard to detect from the beach. There is a large car park below the blockhouse if you decide to drive from St. Laurent.

There is a wealth of memorials in the immediate area of the blockhouse:

Memorial obelisk to the 2nd infantry Division (a reinforcement division ashore on D+1 and 2).

Provisional Engineer Special Brigade Group commemorating all engineer units (located on the outer blockhouse wall behind the obelisk).

The 467th AAA AW Battalion memorial unveiled just before the 50th anniversary in 1994 is above the 50-mm firing aperture (this unit landed at around 0730 hours and quickly lost 28 out of its 36 machine guns). It did, however, knock out the German gun. The memorial plaque to the 467th is appropriately positioned.

Behind the blockhouse there is a grassed track that leads up onto the bluffs. Climb the path and find a suitable site to survey the ground. Face out to sea (due North) Now read on.

The Landing Plan for the 'Big Red One'

Let us now turn our attention to the actions of the 1st Division and initially to the 16th RCT under command of Colonel George Taylor. The plan for the eastern end of Omaha Beach was very similar to that developed for the 29th Division units landing to their west. The 16th Infantry RCT was to land on Easy Red which extends from left to right across your front for 1,850 yards, and Fox Green that starts 1,000 yards to your right. The assault plan projected that the 2nd Battalion Landing Team (BLT) would move off the beach and secure Colleville, approximately 2,400 yards to the southeast. There the 2nd BLT was to establish a blocking position facing south and southeast along the high ground. The 3rd BLT was tasked to gain the plateau and move east clearing German defensive positions before seizing Ste.-Honorine-des-Pertes 4,000 yards away to your right. The 1st BLT was to land and move through the 2nd BLT and secure Formigny at the junction of the D517 and the N13 (4,000 yards southwest). There the BLT was to establish defensive positions astride the N13 overlooking Trevieres and the River Aure and its valley south of the Isigny-Caen road.

It had been planned that the two remaining RCTs of the 1st Division would move through the 16th Infantry beachhead and secure depth objectives. The 18th RCT was scheduled to commence landing at 0930 hours and move across the River Aure to the southeast of Colleville and occupy high ground east of Trevieres and push out patrols to the D-Day objective line 2-3,000 yards south of

LCVPs coming in to land troops on Easy Red.

the N13. Behind them would land the 26th RCT on Corps orders. The 26th RCT was to push east and secure the area around the N13 at Tour-en-Bessin where the Regiment would link-up with 50th British Division coming inland from Gold Beach. As with the 116th Infantry, DD Tanks would support the 16th RCT along with two battalions of artillery equipped with 105-mm howitzers, and the army-navy engineer and demolition teams.

The Initial Landing by 16th RCT

The initial assault wave was launched from the USS *Henrico* and the British *Empire Javelin*. The first wave landings by the 16th RCT were driven off course to the east by the inshore currents. As a result, only two of the twelve boats landed correctly on this mile long sector and they were intermingled with two boats from the 116th RCT, also badly dispersed by the currents and navigation errors. These four boats were fortunate because this sector was in fact only weakly defended. The remainder of Companies E and F landed on Fox Green along with another four disorientated

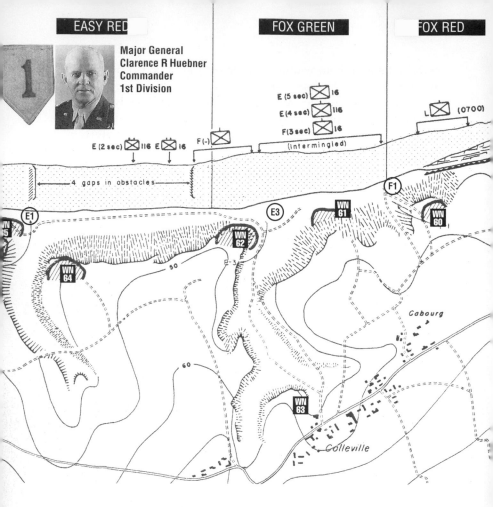

Major General
Clarence R Huebner
Commander
1st Division

E (5 sec) ⊠ 16
E (4 sec) ⊠ 116
F (3 sec) ⊠ 16
(intermingled)

L ⊠ (0700)

E (2 sec) ⊠ 116 E ⊠ 16   F (-) ⊠

F1

4 gaps in obstacles

E1   E3   WN 61   WN 60

WN 62

WN 64   50

60

WN 63

Cabourg

Colleville

boatloads from Company E of the 116th.

Unfortunately for those boats pushed onto Fox Green they were to land inside a series of very well prepared German killing areas. Devoid of even so much as a concrete sea wall for cover, the infantry here faced a similar fate to the hapless Company A of the 116th RCT. The misplaced troops from Company E, 116th RCT paid another heavy 'butcher's bill' on Fox Green. The company had lost its commander and 104 others, 23 of them from a single boatload of 30 troops before the morning was out.

The infantrymen who should have landed on Fox Green were also displaced; Companies I and L of the 3rd BLT had been pushed even further to the east. Company L (less two boats lost on the run-in) landed on Fox Red beyond the F-1 draw. Company I had approached Port-en-Bessin before realizing the error and returning 90 minutes late to land its infantrymen on Fox Green. One lone DD tank, some Shermans that had been landed by LCT directly onto the beach, a navy beach party and 14 boatloads of lost infantry represented the surviving force from the initial assault on Fox Green.

Amongst the early survivors was Lieutenant Commander Joseph P.Vaghi, of the U.S. Naval Reserve. He was the beachmaster – or 'traffic cop' – as he put it, for Easy Red Sector of Omaha Beach. He landed with his platoon C-8 at 0735 hours when the tide was at full-ebb. He and his men had a 500-yard open beach to cross before reaching the cover of the sand dunes. Here is part of his personal account:

'I was the first person to leave the LCI (L) after beaching. The craft had ramps on each side of the bow for purposes of discharging the passengers. Shortly after I left the craft, the right ramp was blown away by an enemy shell which caused numerous casualties, both on the craft and in the water...

My first awareness that what we were doing was real was when an 88-millimetre shell hit our LCI (L) and machine gun fire surrounded us. The Germans were in their pillboxes and bunkers high above the beach on the bluff and had an un-obstructed view of what we were doing.

The atmosphere was depressing. The top of the bluff behind the beach was barely visible; the sound of screeching 12-inch and 14-inch shells from the warships USS Texas *and USS* Arkansas *off shore were new sounds never heard by us before; the stench of expended gunpowder filled the air, and landing craft with rocket launchers moved in close to the shore and spewed forth hundreds of rounds at a time onto the German defences. The sea was rough. Purple smoke emanated from the base of the beach*

Joseph P Vaghi

obstacles as the UDT prepared to detonate another explosive in the effort to clear a path through the obstacles to the dune line – this was the state of affairs as the platoon made its way to the dune line, oh so many yards away.

Using the obstacles as shelter, we moved forward over the tidal flat, fully exposed to machine gun fire. We finally reached the dune

143

line. All of C-8 including Commander Carusi and his staff made the long trek of five hundreds yard safely. God was with us! Three days later, however, Commander Carusi took a bullet through his lung and had to be evacuated. A great leader, to be sure.

Having reached the high water mark, we set about organizing ourselves and planning the next move as we had done so many times during our training period. The principal difference was that we were pinned down – with real machine gun fire – with very little movement to the right or the left of our position and absolutely no movement forward...

I believe the most dramatic event that I experienced that morning was when an Army officer came to me and asked that I, as the beachmaster, pass the word over my powered megaphone that the soldiers were to "move forward". The men of C-8 have speculated that the officer was Colonel George Taylor, who landed at 0830...

After I gave the order, an Army sergeant pushed a 'Bangalore' torpedo through the barbed wire at the top of the dune, exploded it, and opened a gap in the mass of barbed wire. He then turned to his men and said "follow me". He did not order his men forward, but he led them, which was the sign of a leader. The men rushed through the gap onto the flat plateau behind the dune line to the base of the bluff, a distance of some fifty yards or so through heavily mined areas. Many lost their lives or were seriously wounded.

The German strongpoints WN 65 and WN 64 were covering the E-1 draw along with the more dispersed outposts sited along the bluffs. These positions were able to pin down those mixed troops landing

German machine gunners at their deadly work inside one of the *Wiederstandsnest* (WN).

on Easy Red along the beach to your right for some time. At approximately 0830 hours a notable demonstration of individual leadership and heroism took place that is worth recounting. An engineer Lieutenant and a wounded sergeant stood up under fire and walked over to inspect the wire obstacles that were impeding forward movement off the beach. Having assessed the problem the Lieutenant returned to the shingle embankment and looked disgustedly down at the human carpet seeking shelter and said: 'Are you going to lay there and get killed, or get up and do something about it?'

The engineers were to play a significant role in the battle for Easy Red. Here, the strongpoints were to be cleared later in the morning by elements of the 37th and 149th Engineer Combat Battalions working under fire while 2nd Lieutenant John M. Spaulding's section of Company E, 16th RCT manoeuvred up the bluffs and took WN 64 from the rear. The 37th Engineers actually suffered 24 men killed on D-Day including its commanding officer. The unit's contributions to events at the E-1 draw were recognized with the award of three Distinguished Service Crosses for actions taking place within yards of these German fortifications. Two awards went to bulldozer operators who cleared a road through the shingle embankment and dunes above the beach so allowing vehicles to get off the shoreline. This gap was just to the east of the mouth of the draw in the area now occupied by the last house on the right and the prominent track that still leads to the beach to this day. Between 1000 hours and midday these two bulldozer operators then proceeded to fill-in the German antitank ditch that had been dug by the Germans shortly before D-Day across the front of WN 65. This work was taking place as other engineers were clearing mines and obstacles from the draw. This work under fire created the first significant route off Omaha Beach.

The third Distinguished Service Cross went to Lieutenant Robert D. Ross of the 37th for his role in supporting Spaulding's men in their attack on WN 64. During that little battle, 40 Germans were killed and 21 prisoners taken.

He had been fortunate to have intimate fire support from DESRON 18 during his assault and that served to 'soften-up' the position. The destroyers had intervened on Easy Red from about 1000 hours. Two had closed to 1,000 yards to engage German strongpoints from Les Moulins (Dog Red) to Fox Red with heavy accurate fire. This intervention must have cheered the troops still pinned down at the high water mark. In fact at least 5 destroyers closed on this sector to support the 1st division. At 1021 hours the *Frankford*'s Action Report stated 'Fire commenced... and target destroyed.' That target was a pillbox at Exit E-1. At 1036 hours the *Frankford* was again in action, this time against a German mortar battery located on the ridge above E-1. The ship's Action Report stated:

> *'After close observation the exact location of the battery was noted at 1032. At 1036 commenced firing on the battery using direct fire, range about 1200 yards. On the fifth salvo a direct hit was obtained, a large cloud of green smoke was noted and the mortar battery ceased firing. Our troops then advanced and a number of German troops were seen to surrender.'*

Eight minutes later *Frankford* provided further assistance. At 1044 the ship spotted two machine guns covering the E-1 draw and in 12 minutes of fire silenced the offending weapons. Further east the *Harding* was also intervening at a decisive moment. At 1050 hours the ship spotted an enemy pillbox 'which was firing on our troops down draw north of Colleville, thereby delaying operations on the beach. Opened fire on pill box and demolished it.' This kind of intimate fire support provided by DESRON 18 would prove decisive as the day wore on.

By the time reinforcements were arriving from 1000 hours onwards on Easy Red the entrance to the E-1 draw was secure. It had been captured thanks to the excellent cooperation demonstrated by the ships in support of V Corps ground units. However, the German defences were still causing havoc. The 18th RCT had been due to land here at 0930 hours but because of the strong lateral current and congestion both offshore and on the beach, the arrival had been delayed by over 30 minutes. The first craft landed just west of the E-1 draw at about 1000 hours. The 18th RCT had expected to make a safe landing on a benign shore. Unfortunately that would not be the case. Although they did get ashore with only light casualties they lost 28 landing craft to underwater obstacles. With many overloaded men now struggling ashore, one man Private Carlton W. Barrett, took it upon himself to brave the tidal waters and German fire to repeatedly wade into the surf and rescue the wounded and exhausted men floundering in the waves. Barrett then moved the wounded to rescue boats so that they could be evacuated to safety. He excelled that day by also carrying messages along the fire raked beach in addition to caring for the wounded. For his

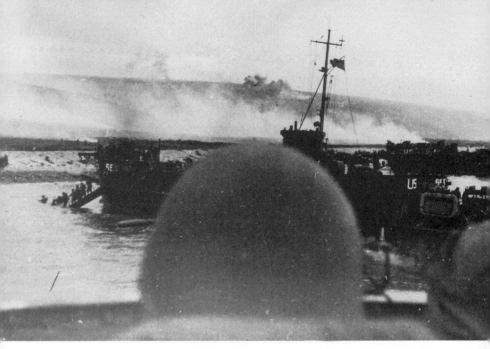

Close support from warships off the beach successfully dealt with
pillboxes. Shells can be seen exploding on the bluff.

courage under fire he was awarded the Congressional Medal of
Honour, the United States' highest award for bravery.

The rest of the 18th RCT was also soon in action. As the Regiment
came ashore the 1st Division's Assistant Commander, Brigadier
General Willard G. Wyman ordered the 18th RCT to take over the
former tasks of the now decimated 16th RCT. Shortly after landing,
the redirected 2nd BLT found a pillbox still occupied and firing on
the beach from the western side of the E-1 draw. Using only tank
support an initial attack failed. A naval shore fire control party then
intervened and contacted a destroyer only 1,000 yards off the beach.
A coordinated fire mission was called for, along with a combined
arms assault being executed by the ground forces. Firing only a few
yards above the crowded beach the ship's fourth round hit the
position and the survivors quickly surrendered. Twenty prisoners
were taken. The offending German bunker was soon reoccupied and
became 'Danger Forward' the forward command post of the 1st
Division. General Huebner would arrive here at 1900 hours on 6th
June.

The entrance to the E-1 draw was now secured. Further close
cooperation between the 18th RCT and the destroyers led to the

clearance of the rest of the St. Laurent draw by 1130 hours. This rapid improvement on Easy Red allowed the surviving units of the Engineer Special Brigade to clear a vehicle exit up the E-1 draw. This became the primary route off the beach on D-Day. Once the offending bunkers had been silenced the engineers also took over the 50-mm casemate (above today's car park) and used it as their command post. On 14th June it would actually receive an official visit from Admiral Harold R. Stark, Commander US Naval Forces Europe during his visit to the beachhead.

As the day progressed the 18th RCT pushed inland over the bluffs to the east of the E-1 draw, this progress hampered by the arrival of the 115th RCT opposite the draw. The 2nd BLT was able to advance via the western edge of Colleville before reaching high ground 600 yards southeast of the village where it established a blocking position for the night. The 1st and 3rd Battalions were also successful in expanding the lodgment. By last light the 1st Battalion had cut the coast road and occupied positions midway between St. Laurent and Colleville after failing to capture the village of Surrain (4,000 yards southeast on the D508). The 3rd BLT had also received a bloody nose against German outposts at Formigny but the BLT by-passed strong resistance and moved to higher ground astride the D514 in an area to the southeast of St. Laurent.

Stand 3: The American National Monument and Cemetery at St. Laurent

Return to your vehicle. If you walked from the village of St. Laurent a recommended route is to rejoin the promenade and walk west towards Vierville for 1600 yards before turning inland and walking up the D517 back to the village. Having rejoined your vehicle **drive to the D514** and **turn left** towards Colleville and Ste. Honorine. The Cemetery is clearly signposted. A detailed route plan and guide to the Cemetery is included in the Appendices.

At the Cemetery move to the northern coastal perimeter path and locate the beach path that descends to the dunes. Examine the map table provided at the top of the path and orientate yourself. Immediately below you is the boundary line between Easy Red and Green. It was to the left of the boundary that the two sections of Company E, 116th and Company E of the 16th RCT landed. Company F used the area astride the boundary to come ashore. To your half-right on Fox Green came the intermingled landings of 3 sections of Company F, 4 sections of Company E of the 116th and 5 sections of Company E from the 16th RCT .

The path from the cemetery to the beach.

* * * * *

At 0810 hours Captain Bill Friedman was approaching the beach at Fox Red. He looked at the all too fast approaching shore and said to his neighbour 'Oh God it looks like Tarawa'. He had recalled the horrific images from the American newsreels of that terrible island battle in the Pacific of November 1943. He remembered images of dead American Marines floating in the surf and the thousand fatal casualties suffered. Was Omaha Beach going to be a repetition of that carnage? He soon leapt into the cold breakers and recalled that 'as the ramp went down the chaos was evident all around us. It looked like God had taken all the debris of the world and thrown it onto that beach'. He went on to recount a lasting image:

'Landing craft on their sides, turned the wrong way... it was like a very strange spectator sport. It was surreal. I had gone off the ramp into deep water. It was up to my chest. As we moved forward I must have been on a ridge of sand because the men around me began to go under and I had to help them stay above the waves. After going about 6 to 8 feet, I felt firm ground beneath me... I then moved quickly to the shingle and just lay down and joined that great big long pile of men on the shale. We were totally immobilized. I did not know what to do, or where to go. I remember looking at the sea and the water was red, there were bodies and equipment just rolling in the surf.'

This was chaos incarnate. He made it to the shingle embankment and caught his breath:

149

'Along the line of men on the shingle I saw people jerking as they were hit with the impact of bullets and shrapnel. Somehow it didn't count. I was reassured because I was shoulder to shoulder with other men. There was something reassuring about having warm, familiar human bodies next to you... even if they were dead... you were not alone... they provided comfort and sometimes even cover from the bullets. At one point I was still lying down and shouting in the ear of the Regimental S4. He was a major. My mouth was next to his ear; it was so noisy that he could not hear me otherwise. While I was trying to make myself understood above the din, a bullet struck him dead. It had hit him in the centre of his helmet... our faces were inches away when it happened... it could have been me.'

Bill Friedman described the effect of this incident in very clear terms: from that moment he realized that there was little that could

be done to change his fate. A few minutes later Colonel Taylor landed with other elements of his headquarters on Fox Red and 'found plenty to do on the beach'. His regimental headquarters was soon established and Taylor set about galvanizing the disorganized troops into action. Directing his men into action he sent forward a single soldier with a 'bangalore' to blow a gap in the wire. The resulting explosion and the appearance of a gap in the obstacle had the desired effect. Thanks to his courageous leadership and example, the men were shaken out of their frozen state and driven to action. From his command post he organized available officers and non-commissioned officers to take patrols inland. By 0830 hours that general infiltration up the bluffs was taking place as small groups of men edged through an increasing number of gaps in the wire and found covered approaches to the crest. As each small team made a penetration they began to inflict casualties on the enemy above them. As each German post was silenced – usually at close quarters with bomb and bullet – more men could move off from the beach, funnelling towards the new gaps in the defences. It was a slow and expensive process.

At about the same time the Navy Beachmaster for Omaha was signalling to all control vessels to cease landing vehicles because of congestion on the beach. The incoming tide and the failure to secure the heavily defended draws had exacerbated that congestion. By that time there were approximately 50 LCT and LCI off the beach

Reinforcements from the 1st Division.

searching for gaps in the obstacles and space to disembark their loads onto the now narrow and evidently over-crowded area. The standoff would continue for 90 minutes. At 0830 hours two young Navy Reserve skippers demonstrated true audacity and courage in the face of the enemy. Lieutenant Sidney W. Brinker on LCT-30 and Lieutenant E.B. Koehler aboard LCI-554 almost simultaneously decided to smash their way to land. With all the ship guns and any assault weapons on the crowded decks that could engage forward, they rammed through to the beach. A destroyer that closed in behind the craft also provided LCI-554 with additional covering fire. LCT-30 grounded opposite E-3 draw with all 20-mm guns blazing at a fortified villa that was being used as part of the WN 62 and WN 63 defenses. The LCT disgorged its cargo onto the shore providing covering fire throughout the process. Inevitably this craft and its audacious crew became a target for 88-mm gun and machine-gun fire. The LCT was soon riddled and had to be abandoned. LCI-554 was more fortunate and made a safe extraction.

Other craft witnessing this courageous and exemplary act now followed suit. A constant flow of troop landings now occurred. Off shore, however, the chaotic situation was only sorted out after 1100 hours when the deputy commanders of Assault Groups 0-1 and 0-2 reorganized the milling landing craft and directed the bulk of landings towards Easy and Fox sectors where movement off the beach had been identified. Before that stage of the battle, Bill Friedman was still enduring the terror on the narrow strip of beach with his friends. Then he witnessed his regimental commander's timely intervention and decisive leadership:

'I was in that mass of living and dead when I saw Colonel Taylor move back from the main line of men and stand up. He started walking up and down the line shouting at the men "move up" and "move out". This had a great effect on me. I remember getting up and starting to shout and scream trying to get the men moving. I didn't hurl myself forward at the defile; I guess that I should have done so. What I did do was urge other men forward.

While doing this, I remember a funny incident on that terrible morning when I approached three soldiers lying down together absolutely rigid. As I did so bodies were being struck by bullets all around us. These three soldiers would not move so I pulled out my pistol and they looked at me, a distraught Captain waving nothing more threatening than his pistol.

I wanted them to go forward to attack up the draw and one of them shouted at me, "Captain are you out of your f...ing mind?"'

2Lt Jack Carroll, Regimental Assistant S-3 in 16/1, also witnessed Colonel Taylor's decisive leadership. He had been sheltering approximately fifteen feet from his commander. He recalled watching Taylor get up and call out to the disorganized, gaggle of men around him,

'Two kinds of people are staying on this beach, the dead and those who are going to die – now lets get the hell out of here!'

With his staff also assisting by example and encouragement, small-improvised teams began to move forward to the bluffs. At about this time Colonel Taylor had

Colonel George Taylor

organized the remaining armour in an attack on the E-3 draw, 400 yards to your right as you face out to sea.

The next obstacle deterring the 1st Division from getting off the beach was an extensive anti-personnel minefield. Bill Friedman recalled moving forward through a gap in the double concertina wire fence with its tripwires and boobytraps and into that minefield. 'It was a moving and dramatic moment'. There were men who had gone ahead, now wounded or limbless, shot by Germans sited in the trenches and bunkers along the top of the bluffs, or blown up by the anti-personnel mines. 'The wounded lay there and pointed out to us where they had trodden, or detonated mines... that was now part of our safe route.' Elsewhere along the beach, Jack Carroll holds a lasting memory of a young officer throwing himself forward onto the ground to clear the last few feet of minefield for his men. A mine detonated and killed him. His men continued the advance over him.

As individuals and small groups reached the base of the escarpment they could find shelter from the devastating enfilade fire from the flanks. Bill Friedman recalled:

'Once we got to the base of the bluffs we were relatively safe. We were quite well protected from view and from the enemy's fire. I don't think that they expected anyone to get off the beach because once we started moving up hill and clearing their positions it became just a matter of time. The positions really did not have any depth to them. That's when I saw my first Germans they were either dead, or already prisoners.'

As the movement off the beach began to gain momentum the Navy continued to provide superb intimate support. Very close to where you are now standing, a German machine gun post was enfilading the beach below. The *Doyle* identified the gun position and fired two salvos from two guns at 1100 hours. The Action Report said:

> *'Target destroyed. Shifted fire to casemate at top of hill, fired two half salvos, target destroyed. Army troops began slow advance up from beach. Manoeuvring ship to stay in position against current which is running at 2.8 knots. Flood tide.'*

For many the beach remained a place of terror and suffering. Pharmacist's Mate Second Class Frank Walden US Navy, was attached to Company C-7 of the 6th Naval Beach Battalion. He was a hospital corpsman assigned to treat the wounded on Omaha Beach. He was attached to an engineer unit for the assault and had to stay on the beach until everything had been landed and the wounded evacuated. He was eighteen years old at the time of the invasion and he was scared to death on 6th June. This is his story:

> *'Although it seemed like one of our many training runs, I think that when we saw bodies floating in the water as we approached the beach, we realized this was to be the real thing. We relied on our training to take over, which it did. During the course of the day I was wounded around 1500.*
>
> *At the time I was wounded, we were pinned down all day and couldn't really do our jobs. We were lying there and a couple of Army medics came by with a fellow on the stretcher. The Germans started to shell the beach and the medics set the stretcher down and an 88-millimetre shell went off and wounded them. Virgil Mount, Corpsman in the 6th Naval Beach Battalion, and I jumped up to treat those two and that's when Virgil was killed and I was wounded. My good friend Don Burroughs was also wounded.*
>
> *Because our beach was closed and we had no way to evacuate, I walked down to the next beach and made it onto an LCT and then to an LST. The LST took me back to England and I was treated there in the hospital and was sent home in September.'*

Stand 4: WN 62 via The Beach Path, Easy Red , and Fox Green

Descend from the Cemetery having used the first orientation table. On the way down the path examine the second orientation depicting the Mulberry Harbour sited at Omaha Beach but destroyed in the great Channel storm on 19th June 1944. As you continue to the base of the bluffs take some time examining the slope and the ground now thick with dense undergrowth. The minor undulations and small gullies provide the clues to the question 'how did anyone get off the beach here?' On reaching the dunes turn right (east) and walk to the E-3 draw where you can join a minor road and turn inland. It was here that the 26th RCT of the 1st Division came ashore and advanced on either side of the draw to establish perimeter positions during the evening of 6th June.

After walking a short distance take the evident path to the right and gain the crest with its magnificent view of Omaha Beach from the eastern flank. Locate the following memorials:

5th Engineer Special Brigade Memorial and plaques to the 20th and 299th Combat Engineers.

The simple and unobtrusive German cross to the men of the coastal defence divisions to the right (east) and rear of WN 62 .

Should you wish to detour into the Village Vacances Familiales you can see the memorial to the 2nd Armoured Division ('Hell on Wheels') and the Memorial Wall and plaques commemorating the749th Tank Battalion.

As you rejoin the road at the end of your visit to WN 62 (the road is a one way circuit and traffic will be approaching you from the rear) head due southwest towards the St. Laurent American Cemetery. After a short distance on your right you will be able to leave the road on a path and visit the 1st Division memorial and obelisk. Having visited this site return to the road and walk back to the Cemetery car park and rejoin your vehicle.

German prisoners being marched off Omaha Beach.

The grim task of collecting and identifying the dead is underway in this picture. Bodies are strapped to stretchers and loaded onto DUKWs to be taken for burial below the bluff. This section of the beach is looking towards Fox Green.

One prominent blockhouse in WN 61 was a Type 677 casemate containing an 88-mm gun just east of E-3 draw on Fox Green. It was actually silenced as early as 0710 hours by a Sherman DD tank commanded by Staff Sergeant Sheppard of the 741st Tank Battalion. The shell-scarred bunker can still be seen on private land above the beach. On the opposite side of the draw were two Type 669 casemates, part of WN 62, each equipped with 75-mm guns. To complete the defences in this area two further 'resistance nests' were sited to cover the F-1 draw. WN 60 (now overgrown) was sited 500 yards east of WN 61. This was the forward observation post of Major Werner Pluskat, the commander of I. Abteilung of Artillerie-

regiment 352. Further to the east of the entrance to the E-3 draw lies Fox Red with its shallow cliffs and rocky outcrops. A small re-entrant, known as the F-1 draw, sits astride the boundary between Fox Green and Fox Red. Further up the E-1 draw, on the spur at the top of the valley at the northern edge of Colleville, was WN 63 in a depth position to cover the exit from the beach. That position is still a bow shaped, wooded crest at the edge of a large field, and would still be defined as an area of key terrain for any approach up the draw from the beach.

It was into the area of the E-3 draw that the divisional reserve would land. At 1300 hours the 26th Infantry Regiment had arrived off the beach in the transport area. By that time the 1st Division had already been notified that troops were at last moving off the beach. As early as 1040 hours the beachmaster on Easy Red had requested,

Vehicles of the 467th Anti-aircraft Artillery Battalion shot up on Omaha. Officially it is recorded that it landed at 8.30 but it is more likely to have been 7.30 when the German defences remained fully effective.

Low tide revealed the full extent of the detritus strewn over the beaches

'send in H+195 wave at once.' By 1137 hours the divisional headquarters had been informed that 'Germans [were] reported leaving positions and surrendering to American soldiers.' At 1341 hours the divisional G-3 journal recorded a positive message from the Navy:

> 'Beaches DOG GREEN WHITE RED are entirely clear of opposition and ready for landing trs. No opposition on beach. EASY GREEN and RED tps ashore apparently waiting infantry reinforcements. All fire support ships are waiting on Army for target assignments.'

It is ironic that Bradley was considering ordering a withdrawal from Omaha and Eisenhower was trying to get a bomber force to attack the beach area at the very time that the tide was turning for the 'thin wet line of khaki that dragged itself ashore'. In reality, the generals off the beach were wholly out of control of events ashore. It fell to the Assistant Divisional Commanders – Cota and Wyman – to provide real tactical command and leadership. The actual conduct of the battle itself then fell to the individual soldiers of all ranks who were prepared to take the fight to the enemy. Many sacrificed themselves in doing so. Others relieved their shock and horror of events on the beach upon the enemy.

When the 26th RCT began to land at about 1800 hours on Fox Green Brigadier General Wyman ordered the 1st BLT to help shore up the depleted 16th Infantry's left flank. As a result, this fresh battalion only had to advance about a thousand yards to get into

position on the high ground on the eastern side of the E-3 draw. There they took up positions in front of the German strongpoint in the village at Cabourg. Within three hours the rest of the Regiment was ashore. Wyman inserted the 2nd and 3rd BLTs into the line beyond the St. Laurent - Colleville road between the 115th RCT and the 18th RCT where they were poised to expand the beachhead the following morning.

The Enemy Situation

As German positions along the bluffs were cut off or destroyed, many retreating soldiers fell victim to understandably ruthless American ambushes. Many Germans were unaware of the location of friendly or enemy troops as the situation rapidly deteriorated. When Lieutenant Frerking ordered WN 62 to be evacuated it had already been outflanked. His last request for fire was dramatic: 'Gunfire barrage on the beach. Every shell a certain hit. We are getting out.' With enemy tanks now firing on their bunker complex, his men slipped away to the south from cover to cover, in search of safety. By the time one of his machine gunners and a signaller had made it back to the command post of the 1st Battalion the 726th Regiment, just north of Colleville, the rest of the group, including Frerking, were already dead.

Local German counter-attacks were launched amidst this confused intermingling of American and German forces. In truth, confusion became the common characteristic of the events above the beach as American detachments pushed inland with by-passed German groups also attempting to move back from the shore. By 1140 hours Lieutenant Spaulding had reached the southwest exit from Colleville with his Company G of the 16th RCT. There he observed several groups of German troops moving towards the village from the north. In the absence of radio communications with his battalion and regiment he was reliant on runners to keep the links open. He recalled seeing one of his own company runners get killed by one German group:

> 'After he fell they fired at least 100 rounds of MG [machinegun] ammunition into him. It was terrible but we do the same thing when we want to stop a runner from taking information. Of course we didn't find out what he was coming to tell us.'

Colleville would actually change hands several times that day. The Infantry Regiment 726 and elements of 352nd Division each tried in vain to counter-attack and re-secure the village as a blocking position against further American expansion from the shallow beachhead. Given the village's critical location at the head of the E-3 and F-1 draws it certainly was vital ground to both defender and attacker alike. But in the absence of a concentrated, powerful and well-coordinated counter-attack there was little hope of driving the Americans back into the sea even at this early stage.

CHAPTER SEVEN

EPILOGUE

AT THE GOING DOWN OF THE SUN

The German Perspective: Rommel's 'Longest Day'

During the early hours of the morning on 6th June General Marcks had alerted headquarters 7th Army in Le Mans. He realized that the airborne operations being reported from the Cotentin to the River Dives east of Caen represented the initial stages of an amphibious operation. Thereafter, 7th Army notified Army Group B and OB West. During this critical period Rommel, was absent from his headquarters at La Roche Guyon. He was actually in Stuttgart where he was celebrating his wife's birthday before going on to meet Hitler at Berchtesgaden on 6th June. The Field Marshal did not learn of the invasion until 1015 hours when his Chief of Staff, Major

General Hans Spiedel – an opponent and plotter against Hitler – informed him by phone. His response was to question Spiedel as to the status of OB West's armoured reserves. Hearing that Hitler had not as yet released them, he simply stated 'How stupid of me,' and set about returning to France.

At the strategic level Adolf Hitler had responded to the news of the invasion with total assurance that his plans and preparations were complete. When his Chief of operations, General Jodl had finally notified him of the invasion he declared, with a radiant smile on his face, 'It's begun at last.' During the early hours of 6th June Jodl had not even bothered to wake Hitler from his sleep to present the fateful report

Hitler and his Chief of Operations General Jodl. Upon receiving news of the invasion from Jodl Hitler responded with a radiant 'It's begun at last".

from OB West. By doing this Jodl imposed several hours delay on the release of the panzer reserves to the operational and tactical commanders in France. Having accepted the news with total sang-froid, Hitler then went to a reception for the new Hungarian Prime Minister in Salzburg.

Throughout OB West the German response was confused, inappropriate and piecemeal. This was due in part to the Bodyguard operations drawing the eyes and thoughts of the German High Command to the Pas de Calais. It was also due to a combination of factors that created enormous frictions in the gears of OB West. As Carl Von Clausewitz wrote in his thesis *On War* over a century earlier:

'Four elements make up the climate of war: danger, physical exertion, intelligence and friction, are the elements that form the atmosphere of war and turn it into a medium that impedes activity.'

The friction referred to by Clausewitz is present in any human activity but most particularly in war. In 1944 the German high command had managed to further impede the ability of its local commanders in Normandy to make effective decisions and execute optimal plans in a timely manner. The absence of any concept of joint operations was particularly evident when the Luftwaffe and German Navy failed to co-ordinate their defensive plans and integrate their command structures with Army Group B and OB West . This weakness was highlighted when they failed to intervene in any significant manner before and during D-Day.

Even within the German land component itself, there was a disunity that could only contribute to the Allied cause. Information was not passed throughout the commands as the threat emerged in the early morning of 6th June. German coastal stations had detected and reported activity at sea east of Cherbourg and north of Caen by 0250 hours yet no detailed assessment reached Corps then or later. It was not until 0900 hours that General Marcks 84th Corps notified Army that major landings were taking place. The naval bombardment reported to Army Group B was assessed as being part of a diversionary operation. The Corps staff believed that the situation was more threatening to the north of Caen. Rommel's headquarters endorsed this analysis.

The situation in the Cotentin and the Omaha sector did not cause much concern throughout the day and little attention was paid to the reported events west of Bayeux. The landings by the 82nd and 101st Airborne Divisions were assumed to be part of an elaborate deception. This misappreciation of the situation continued until late afternoon and early evening when the reports became more accurate. The amphibious landings by an enemy division on Utah Beach and the rapid collapse of the La Madelaine defences were clearly the actions of a link-up force for the airborne troops inland.

At 1800 hours the 352nd Division reported the grim situation with some accuracy. Allied forces were reported infiltrating through gaps in the belt of coastal strongpoints and armour had now reached a line from Colleville to Louvieres and Asnieres. The objective of this attack was assessed as being the historic city of Bayeux. On the 352nd Division's eastern flank British forces were reported pushing inland from Le Hamel and la Riviere (Gold Beach) successfully overrunning defensive positions and threatening the Caen-Bayeux road. As a result of so much inaccurate reporting and with inadequate mobile reserves, the Germans focus of attention remained in the east of the lodgment area. Defeating the threat to Caen remained the priority.

During the early hours of the 6th June the 21st Panzer Division had been launched piecemeal towards the airborne forces astride the Orne. Later in the day, after hours of wasted time responding to order and counter-order, the tank regiment of the 21st Panzer Division was launched into the gap between Juno and Sword sectors north of Caen. Marcks personally supervised the attack and launched its commander, Oberst Von Oppeln-Bronikowski, into battle with a dire warning: 'Oppeln, if you don't succeed in throwing the British into the sea, we shall have lost the war.' The assault was quickly smashed against a well-sited anti-tank screen and a perfectly positioned British armoured regiment on high ground south of Sword Beach.

Back towards Omaha Beach Marcks' Corps Headquarters had notified Army that amphibious landings from the Vire estuary to Bayeux had been defeated. It was not until 1640 hours that a more accurate assessment began to reach Army and Army Group headquarters and by then the available reserves had already been committed.

The next days would be characterized by an increasingly desperate attempt to bring up the I SS Panzer Corps and mount a co-ordinated armoured counter-attack in the Caen sector. As the German land-line communications network collapsed under air, naval bombardment and resistance operations radio communications increased allowing the Ultra organization at Bletchley Park to take a more active role in monitoring and identifying the move of the critical reserves towards Normandy.

In the days following D-Day one of Ultra's most significant contributions to the success of Neptune-Overlord was the identification of Headquarters Panzer Group West at a critical moment when it was about to co-ordinate a significant armoured thrust at the beachheads. In a near perfect example of a reconnaissance-strike operation, Geyr Von Schweppenburg's command group was detected, identified and recognized and within hours attacked by Mitchell bombers and rocket firing Typhoons. At 0920 hours on 11th June the telephone log at German 7th Army Headquarters recorded:

'G-3 [probably 7th Army] *informs G-3 Army Group B that... the Panzer Group West has been knocked out by a direct hit on its Headquarters. Command has been give to the First* [SS] *Panzer Corps.'*

V Corps and the 1st Division at the End of the Day

The 1st Division had demonstrated an admirable resilience to the effects of battlefield dislocation and disruption. The fighting qualities of the division are clearly worthy of note. This was a well-

The logistic build-up begins. Note the horseshoe shape of Omaha Beach. This was a defender's dream.

motivated, well lead, and effectively trained force. High morale and esprit de corps had created powerful bonds between the men. Nor was this an inferior, inflexible, organization driven by doctrine and dogma. This was not a formation that fought its battles with just materiel. Individual groups had performed 'like commandos,' as Jack Carroll described their performance that day. Nor were junior commanders devoid of initiative or the willingness to execute the plan and head for their objective in the absence of flanking units or higher leadership. This capability was displayed by so many men in the 1st Division – and the 2nd/5th Rangers – that this alone is reason enough for Eisenhower's effusive compliments to the Division after the battle.

It was not until late afternoon that a semblance of regimental command and control would be established beyond the beach and even then the situation remained confused. The key now was to establish a secure front line that could hold any further counter-attacks and provide security to the ongoing landing operations onto the debris-strewn beach. At 1705 hours Major General Gerhardt came ashore and established his command post in the Vierville

draw in a small quarry. With unit liaison officers and Norman Cota updating him, he re-assumed command of the 29th Division and formulated his plans for the next day. That night he dismissed all words of pessimism. Subsequently, in the 29th Division's report on the invasion entitled 'Battle Lessons and Conclusions' he stated:

'No reports of disaster should be allowed. THEY ARE NEVER TRUE.'

At 1900 hours that night the V Corps headquarters also came ashore and established its command post above the E-1 draw. General Gerow arrived there an hour later and his first message to General Bradley read: 'Thank God for the United States Navy.' This was a testament to the decisive close support provided by DESRON 18 to the assault troops.

As the evening wore on the destroyers kept on station being engaged by the few surviving German gun positions in Port en Bessin and between Vierville and Pointe du Hoc. Generally, after a return salvo from the bombardment force or the 5-inch or 40-mm guns of the destroyers, these threats were silenced. At sunset that night (2206 hours) the naval guns also fell silent. Ashore, sporadic bursts of small arms fire broke the night as nervous troops on either side engaged shadows or caught enemy stragglers and patrols in ambushes. The sound of shouts of 'Fire in hole' and a dull crump of TNT could also be heard above the beach as soldiers blew foxholes for shelter for the night. Conditions remained chaotic in the beachhead as detachments and individual survivors tried to find their parent units, a process that would continue for the next few days. Captain Bill Friedman S-1, 16 RCT, had survived the ordeal on the beach and he recalled that:

'For the next two days we pretty much just licked our wounds and tried to find out who was alive. We now had to reconstruct the Regiment. I recall the endless reports that I had to complete and the arrival of the fresh reinforcements. I also recall that I was under cover somewhere around Colleville, it was quiet and I was not under fire.'

That night between St. Laurent and Colleville, and beyond the coast road to the south, units from four regiments would hold the line. Colleville was still in German hands but virtually encircled. St. Laurent was partially secured from the east up to the main crossroads in the village. Vierville was completely secure with leading units from 116th pushing south towards Louvieres and west towards the isolated Rangers at Pointe du Hoc .

Bill Friedman was dispatched to find headquarters 1st Division

Following D-Day landing craft could begin bringing in stores and reinforcements. Use of anti-aircraft balloons had to be dicontinued as German guns inland used their position to zero in on the beaches. Note the German anti-tank ditch this side of the trenches (below).

during the evening of D-Day. His account of his meeting with Huebner is worthy of recording here:

'Colonel Taylor sent me to find General Huebner about the time that the 18th RCT began to move up. I found the General and I said "Colonel Taylor sends his respects," and presented my report. The general had tears in his eyes and all he could say was "you did it...you did it!" He was deeply moved by the all too-evident sacrifice. Later that night I fell asleep in a farmyard around Colleville. I recall a sense of being purged.

I had been frightened in battle before D-Day and again many times afterwards. But that day I was not frightened. I was simply convinced that we had absolutely no influence or control over our fate. No action we could take would have stopped a bullet. It was surreal.

When I was awakened next morning it was by French women who gave me some Camembert cheese to eat and Calvados to drink. I had survived D-Day.'

At the end of the day they were ashore, short of their objectives, but ashore. None of the Overlord assault divisions had achieved their missions in full, however, they had all successfully breached Hitler's *Festung Europa*. The Allies had executed a complex plan with its many interdependent and intricate parts. They had also landed a substantial force with such effect that the Germans would not be able to dislodge them. Each side now rushed to build up forces and materiel in Normandy in order to establish a cohesive front line. However, in the forthcoming days the Allies and the Germans would both miss opportunities for decisive action and so condemn their armies to a gruelling war of attrition that would last into August.

OMAHA Sector in Perspective: In the Footsteps of Warriors

Look down upon the beach from the cemetery at St. Laurent. Ponder the sacrifice of so many young men. Imagine their fear and sense of duty as they approached the hostile shore on that cold, wet Tuesday morning on 6 June 1944. Many of them never reached the high water mark. They were cut down in their assault craft, drowned in unseaworthy tanks, or fell victim to German fire on the wide-open beach flats. Their youth and their fear remain two constants of any army in any conflict.

The resolution of the men in Force Omaha is now legend.

Wounded GIs on their way back to England.

Coast Guardsman with prisoners from the Ost Battalion (East Battalion), 716th Division – some of the defenders of Omaha. Recruited into the German army from among Russian prisoners of war. They would be returned to the Soviet Union following the end of hostilities almost certainly to be executed.

Individuals such as Colonel George Taylor, Norman Cota, Joe Dawson and John Finke all contributed to getting their men out of those harrowing killing areas along the seashore and up the bluffs to relative safety. There, they could prosecute the assault plan and clear the Germans from their seemingly impregnable positions. In many instances little quarter was given and one suspects that little was expected. The sailors and Coast Guard crews also endured the horror. Seth Shepard was a young crewman on LCI (L) 92 his account was written at a 'survivors base', Plymouth on 25 June 1944:

'Shocked and exhausted we crawled out of the sea over the smooth pebbles of the Normandy beach a few hours after the start of the great invasion of June 6. Around us as we sank upon the stones were dead and dying American soldiers and sailors; behind us the windswept sea broke against our burning ship; ahead of us in the hills German snipers and machine guns raked the beach. Through it all the deadly 88s and exploding mines blasted the land and sea approaches shattering the beach and water with violent concussions and filling the gray skies with heavy smoke.

I was with this veteran... Coast Guard crew through... those 16 hours of tortuous waiting after our ship – the Coast Guard manned LCI (L) 92 – struck two deadly mines in swift succession, followed by direct hits from German 88s. It was the worst hell the crew had ever experienced in four major invasions. We faced death and destruction so often that day that the first shock of abandoning our burning ship under heavy fire was overcome in constant German shelling the whole time we lay there wet, cold and scared without weapons, warm clothes, or food other than a few cans of soup and Army blankets.'

Shepard's account demon-

Royal Military Police keep a watchful eye on prisoners taken during the D-Day operations as they disembark in England.

173

Mulberry Harbour system at Omaha.

strates the very personal realities of battle. A visit to Normandy will invariably bring out other human factors that decide battlefield success or failure. Consider the importance of decision-making under stress. Ponder on the leadership, organizational skills, principles of war, and the many countless battlefield variables that determined the outcome of this mighty endeavour. Without the leadership of two brigadier generals and a handful of relatively junior officers and soldiers, or the courageous intervention of the American destroyer squadron on the morning of D-Day, the story of Omaha Beach would be as tragic as the history of the Dieppe Raid in 1942.

Today the surviving veterans of Omaha Beach recall the events of half a century ago with startling clarity. Their memories of the first hours on the beach and the fighting inland in the bocage are crisp and clear, etched on their minds. Many of these venerable gentlemen even now recount their impressions with emotion.

Ambulances bring wounded out to a hospital ship before the Channel storm that destroyed the harbour.

The Omaha harbour, 'Mulberry A', is smashed up in the storm of 19 June – this led to its being abandoned.

One of the most poignant and lasting memoirs of Omaha Beach can be found in the columns of Ernie Pyle's reports to the Scripps-Howard newspapers. Between the 7-9 June he wrote three powerful, evocative pieces based on his walk along the beach on D+1. Read this as you sit, or promenade at leisure on the sands of Omaha where the terrain endures though the scars of that bloody day in June 1944 have healed:

'I took a walk along the historic coast of Normandy in the country of France.

It was a lovely day for strolling along the seashore. Men were sleeping on the sand, some of them sleeping forever. Men were floating in the water, but they didn't know they were in the water, for they were dead...

I walked for a mile and a half along the water's edge of our many miled invasion beach. You wanted to walk slowly, for the detail on that beach was infinite.

The wreckage was vast and startling. The awful waste and destruction of war, even aside from the loss of human life, has always been one of its outstanding features to those who are in it. Anything and everything is expendable. And we did expend on our beachhead in Normandy during those first few hours...

But there is another and more human litter. It extends in a thin line, just like a high-water mark, for miles along the beach. This is the strewn personal gear, gear that will never be needed again, of those who fought and died to give us our entrance into Europe.

Here in a jumbled row for mile on mile are soldiers' packs. Here are socks and shoe polish, sewing kits, diaries, Bibles and hand grenades. Here are the latest letters from home, with the address on each one neatly razored out – one of the security precautions enforced before the boys embarked.

Here are toothbrushes and razors, and snapshots of families back home staring at you from the sand. Here are pocket books, metal mirrors, extra trousers, and bloody abandoned shoes. Here are broken

177

handled shovels, and portable radios smashed almost beyond recognition...

I stepped over the form of one youngster whom I thought was dead. But when I looked down I saw he was only sleeping. He was very young and very tired. He lay on one elbow, his hand suspended in the air about six inches from the ground. And in the palm of his hand he held a large, smooth rock.

I stood and looked at him a long time. He seemed in his sleep to hold that rock lovingly, as though it was his last link with a vanishing world...

The strong, swirling tides of the Normandy coastline shift the contours of the sandy beach as they move in and out. They carry soldiers' bodies out to sea, and later return them. They cover the corpses of heroes with sand, and then in their whims they uncover them.

As I plowed out over the wet sand of the beach...I walked around what seemed to be a couple of pieces of driftwood sticking out of the sand. But they weren't driftwood.

They were a soldier's two feet...The toes of his G.I. shoes pointed towards the land he had come so far to see, and which he saw so briefly.'

General Eisenhower summarized the events at Omaha Beach in his official report on Operation Neptune-Overlord. He stated that:

'It was in the St. Laurent-sur-Mer sector, on Omaha Beach, where the American V Corps' assault was launched, that the greatest difficulties were experienced. Not only were the surf conditions worse than elsewhere, causing heavy losses in amphibious tanks and landing craft among the mined obstacles, but the leading formations...had the misfortune to encounter at the beach the additional strength of... the 352nd Infantry, which had recently reinforced the coastal garrison... Exhausted and disorganized at the edge of the pounding breakers, the Americans were at first pinned to the beaches but, despite a murderous fire from the German field guns along the cliffs, with extreme gallantry, they worked their way through the enemy positions. The cost was heavy... but by their unflinching courage, they turned what might have been a catastrophe into a glorious victory.'

SELECTIVE BIBLIOGRAPHY

Ambrose, Stephen E., *D-Day June 6, 1944:The Climactic Battle of World War II*, New York, 1994.

Balkoski, Joseph, *Beyond the Beachhead*, Harrisburg, 1989.

Bennett, Ralph, *Ultra in the West*, London, 1979.

Bradley, Omar, *A Soldier's Story*, London, 1952.

Cruikshank, Charles, *Deception in World War II*, Oxford, 1979.

D'Este, Carlo, *Decision in Normandy*, London, 1983.

Foote Finke, Blythe, *No Mission Too Difficult*, Chicago, CB, 1995.

Guderian, Heinz, *Panzer Leader*, London, 1952.

Harrison, G. A., *US Army in World War II. Cross Channel Attack*, Washington, 1951.

Hinsley, Prof. F. H., & others, *British Intelligence in the Second World War*, vol. ii, London, 1979.

Kershaw, Robert J, *D-Day Piercing the Atlantic Wall*, Annapolis, 1994.

Kirkland Jr., William B. *Destroyers at Normandy*, Washington; 1994.

Man, John, *The D-Day Atlas*, New York, 1994.

Prados, Edward F, *Neptunus Rex*, Novato, 1998.

Ramsey, Winston G., *D-Day Then and Now*, London, 1995.

Spiedel, Hans, *We Defended Normandy*, London, 1951.

Tobin, James, *Ernie Pyle's War*, Kansas, 1997.

Warlimont, Walter, *Inside Hitler's Headquarters*, London, 1962.

APPENDIX A:

The Lessons Learnt from Operation Jubilee

Part V

1.The Lessons in Summarized Form

324. The need for overwhelming fire support, including close support during the final stages of the attack.

325. The necessity for the formation of permanent naval assault forces with a coherence comparable to that of any other first line fighting formation. Army formations intended for amphibious assaults must without question be trained in close co-operation with such naval assault forces.

326. The necessity for planning a combined operation at a Combined Headquarters where the Force Commanders and their staff can work and live together.

327. The necessity to plan a raid so as to be independent of weather conditions in the greatest possible degree. A plan based on the assumption that weather conditions will be uniform is very likely to fail; therefore a plan which can be carried out even when they are indifferent or bad is essential.

328. The necessity for flexibility in the military plan and its execution.

To achieve this, the assault must be on the widest possible front limited only by the possibilities of control and the amount of naval and air support available.

329. The allocation to the assault of the minimum force required for success and the retention of the maximum force as a reserve to exploit success where it is achieved.

330. The necessity for as accurate and as comprehensive a system of control and communication as it is possible to establish.

331. The dissemination of knowledge to officers and other ranks, each of whom should know the intention of his superior, the outline of the operation and the details of the task of his own unit and those on the flanks.

332. The value of special training, particularly in amphibious night operations. Such training must include rehearsals and the testing of inter-communications arrangements.

333. The necessity for fire support in any operation where it has not been possible to rely on the element of surprise. The fire support must be provided by heavy and medium Naval bombardment, by air action, by special vessels or craft working close inshore, and by using the fire power of the assaulting troops while still sea-borne. Special close-support craft, which should be gun-boats or some form of mobile fort, do not exist and must be designed and constructed.

Support by the Royal Air Force is effective within the limits imposed by time and space.

334. Assaults must be carefully timed. Whether to assault in darkness, at dawn or dusk or in daylight, must depend on the nature of the raid, and on certain conditions, such as tide and distance, which will vary in every case.

335. Tanks should not be landed until the anti-tank defences have been destroyed or cleared. L.C.T carrying tanks must not linger on the beaches beyond the time required to disembark their loads.

336. Great and continuous attention must be paid to security problems and greater use made of subordinate officers who should be put partly into the picture, so that they can control the men under them. Only important extracts from the Operations Orders should be taken ashore. These should be kept in manuscript form and have their official headings removed.

337. Briefing of the troops should take place as late as possible.

If airborne troops are used, arrangements must be made to increase the number of models available so as to cut down the time needed for briefing.

Airborne troops provide means of achieving surprise and should be used as often as possible subject to the limitations of the weather. It should be regarded, however, as exceptional for a plan to depend for success entirely on their use.

338. Unless means for the provisions of overwhelming close support are available, assaults should be planned to develop round the flanks of a strongly defended locality rather than frontally against it.

339. A far higher standard of aircraft recognition is essential both in the Royal Navy and the Army. This should be achieved by means of lectures, photographs and silhouettes. If possible, personnel of the Royal Observer Corps should be carried in ships.

340. Beach Signal parties should not land complete with the first wave, but only when the beach has been secured.

341. The importance and necessity of using smoke cannot be over emphasized and larger quantities of smoke must be carried in any operation of the size of the assault on Dieppe.

342. Some form of light or self-propelled artillery must be provided once an assault has got across the landing place and is making progress inland.

APPENDIX B:

Points for Discussion at Omaha Beach and Pointe du Hoc

The Plan:

a. Was the Neptune-Overlord Plan correct in focusing V US Corps onto such an exposed and easily defended beach area?

b. Was the intelligence assessment of the defences sufficiently adequate to give the assault battalions the guidance needed?

c. Why was it considered viable that the exposed assault battalions would overcome the defences with the aid of the DD tanks?

German Defences and Allied Intelligence:

a. The Allies had an astonishingly detailed picture of German defences. Could anything have been done to improve the plan for a frontal assault at Omaha Beach had the V Corps had more warning of the presence of 352 Division?

b. Could the Allies have avoided the need for the Ranger operations against Pointe du Hoc given the available reconnaissance technology and up to date intelligence from the French Resistance?

The Bombardment Plan and Execution:

a. How could the air bombardment plan have been improved?

b. Why was the initial naval bombardment ineffective?

The Impact of Friction:

a. Friction in war takes many forms. General Bradley was an experienced soldier yet he rejected advice and the lessons from the Pacific campaign. General Marshall had seconded Major General Charles Corlett from the Pacific Theater to Bradley's headquarters. Corlett had witnessed two major amphibious assaults and yet General Bradley dismissed this assistance as 'bush league' warfare. Can lessons learned be transferred from theater to theater? Would amphibious 'Alligators' have reduced the casualties suffered by the infantry and engineer companies?

The Assault Landing:

a. Given the less than ideal sea state off Omaha Beach could the amphibious landing plan have been adapted by the local commander?

b. What could have been done to increase the chances of getting the DD Tanks and DUKWs carrying the artillery units ashore?

Consider a range of reasons for the high casualties suffered by the initial waves at Omaha Beach?

American Equipment:

a. Bradley rejected the use of the British 79th Armoured Division's specialized armour or 'Funnies.' He cited the Americans' lack of familiarity with this untried and unblooded equipment as his reason. Could the 'Funnies' have helped break through the German defences during the first few hours?

Command and Control:
a. Consider the command and control complexities of splitting the assault area into a two-regiment frontage from two separate divisions? The alternative would have been to put the experienced 1st Division onto the beach with two seasoned and interoperable regiments in the initial wave.
b. What mechanisms enabled the afloat commanders to gather a clearer picture of conditions on the beach? What action was taken to support the troops ashore?

Leadership in Battle:
a. What made the troops formerly pinned down on Omaha Beach take the battle to their enemy?
b. Identify the important characteristics of different leaders under such terrible and demanding conditions?

Service Interoperability:
a. The Allies benefited from a joint and combined philosophy. How had that evolved during the war?
b. Assess Lord Louis Moutbatten's contribution to establishing an effective Combined Operations Headquarters. Was this an important factor in the outcome of D-Day and the crucial battle at Omaha Beach?

Contrast the following strengths and weaknesses and consider their importance to the outcome of Operation Neptune:

Allies' Strengths:
     Air superiority.
     Command of the sea.
     Fully resourced and effective deception plans.
     Surprise (a principle of war).
     Excellent intelligence at the strategic, operational and tactical levels.
     Industrial power and innovative development of specialized equipment
     Use of airborne forces to shatter enemy cohesion.
     Superior leadership and command and control.
German weaknesses:
     A divided and confused command and control system.
     Over reliance on fixed fortifications.
     Lack of accurate intelligence and weather forecasting.
     Lack of air and naval forces capable of operating together or independently.

APPENDIX C:

SOME RECOMMENDED MUSEUMS

Bayeux. Musée de la Bataille de Normandie, Boulevard Fabian Ware (Tel: 02 31 92 93 41), provides an excellent overview of the Battle for Normandy up to the closure of the Falaise Pocket in August 1944. A 30-minute film is shown in French and English (admission fee).

Across the street is the Commonwealth War Graves Commission Cemetery (CWGC) containing 4,648 graves. This is the largest British World War II cemetery in France. Opposite the entrance is the Memorial to the Missing.

While in Bayeux it is worth visiting the Centre Guillaume le Conquérant (admission fee) and viewing the Bayeux Tapestry on rue de Nesmond (Tel: 02 31 51 25 50).

Arromanches. Musée du Debarquement (Tel: 02 31 22 34 31) located on the promenade in the centre of town (admission fee). Excellent view and explanation of the Mulberry Harbour complex still visible offshore over half a century after its construction to protect Port Winston.

Caen Memorial: Un Musée pour la Paix (Tel: 02 31 06 06 44) inaugerated in 1988. The museum has only limited exhibits but provides a dramatic audio-visual display of the war and the liberation. There is a substantial research facility and excellent bookshop (entrance fee).

Grandcamp. Located on the promenade the Rangers Museum (02 31 92 33 51) has a small display and film presentation (entrance fee).

APPENDIX D:

THE NORMANDY AMERICAN NATIONAL CEMETERY AND MEMORIAL AT St. LAURENT

The Normandy American National Military Cemetery and Memorial at St. Laurent is located on the bluffs above the eastern end of Omaha Beach. The site is well signposted and can be reached by car from the D.514; this is the coast road from Isigny-sur-Mer to Caen. The distance from some local cities are: Le Havre, 94 miles/152 kms.; Caen, 29 miles/46 kms. And Cherbourg, 50 miles/81 kms. Adequate hotel and chambre d'hote accommodation is available in the immediate vicinity, particularly in Port en Bessin and Bayeux.

The Cemetery can also be reached directly from the beach via the steep 'S' shaped path that starts at the base of the bluffs on Easy Red. In the winter months, or during a frost, the path can become slippery. During particularly wet periods, the salt marsh between the dunes and the bluffs can also flood the lower reaches of the path and so deter all walkers except for the hardy, or well prepared. A convenient car park for walkers is located at the beach entrance to the E-1 draw beyond the western boundary of the memorial site. Here, just above the car park, is WN 65 centred on the strongpoint's remaining Type 665 casemate, with a 50mm cannon still dominating Easy Red. The prolific memorials in this area are described in more detail below. If the weather permits, this approach to the Cemetery is highly recommended.

This impressive cemetery covers a site of 172 acres and is now maintained by the American Battle Monuments Commission. There are 9,814 burials here. Of those, 307 are unidentified and their stones bear the following inscription: 'Here rests in honored glory a comrade in arms known but to God.' A total of 1,557 Americans were either never found, or if found, their bodies could not be identified. Their names are inscribed on the semi-circular wall in the American Garden of the Missing. Note the inscription towards the rear of this memorial:

'TO THESE WE OWE THE HIGH RESOLVE THAT THE
CAUSE FOR WHICH THEY DIED SHALL LIVE.'

This statement is an extract from General Eisenhower's dedication contained in the American Roll of Honor in St. Paul's

185

Cathedral, London.

By June 10, 1944 the American graves registration companies had established eight cemeteries in the Omaha and Utah beachheads. This equated to one per division. Within the month the cemeteries had been reorganized and concentrated at five main locations: No.1 Cemetery at St. Laurent , La Cambe, Blosville, Orglandes, and Ste. Mere Eglise. Memorial stones now mark these sites. After the war, the U.S. authorities established 'Area Cemeteries' that were approved by Congress in 1947. The one for Normandy remained at St. Laurent. During this process, the American Government at the request of families and next of kin repatriated a total of over 14,000 remains.

Individual burials are adorned with either a white marble cross (Christian, Muslim, or a Star of David). Each stone bears the unit, name, and rank, date of death and State of the deceased serviceman. Some head stones are engraved with gold lettering. These indicate the resting place of recipients of the Medal of Honor. Of particular note is Brigadier General Theodore Roosevelt. He lies in Plot D, Row28, Grave 45. Please note that beside him lies his younger brother Lieutenant Quentin Roosevelt who died in France in 1918. He was re-interred at St. Laurent after the Cemetery was established in 1956.

Cemetery Office. The very efficient Cemetery and Memorial office may be contacted on Tel; 331 22 40 62. The Visitors Building (to the left of the main entrance) provides access to the cemetery registers, literature and postcards of this and other American Battle Monument sites.

The Memorial. Walk into the cemetery and on the right will be found the dignified, semi-circular colonnade with its engraved and enamelled battle maps, memorial bell and urns. A central 22 foot bronze statue represents the 'Spirit of Youth Rising from the Waves'.

Garden of the Missing. This is located behind the Memorial.

Reflective Pool. To the left of the Memorial lies the Reflective Pool. On a clear, bright day a beautiful image can be captured as the water mirrors the elegant Memorial, the flags and statuary amongst its water lilies.

Chapel. Follow the central pathway to the non-denominational chapel. There are two spectacular mosaics: the first depicts 'America' blessing her sons as they leave to fight for freedom in France and 'France' commemorating America's sacrifice with a wreath. When visiting the chapel, consider the words engraved upon the wall: 'Think not upon their passing — remember the glory of their spirit.' Many veterans have never forgotten the friends and colleagues left behind at Omaha Beach.

The Beach Path. Along the northern perimeter of the Cemetery runs a broad, shaded path. It provides a wonderful view across the dunes to the sea. Along this path, and close to the Memorial, can be found an orientation table illustrating the landing beaches. From here one can join the path down the bluffs to the beach. A second orientation table further down the bluffs illustrates the layout of the Mulberry Harbour that was shattered by the great storm of 19 June 1944. At the base of the bluffs the path crosses the salt marsh which can flood in the winter and prevent walkers making a dry crossing to the dunes.

APPENDIX E:

THE GERMAN CEMETERY AT LA CAMBE

The German Cemetery at La Cambe is well signposted and located on the south side of the N13 between Bayeux and Isigny-sur-Mer . The German Cemetery lies upon historic ground. On 23 July 1944, after the bloody battle for St. Lô the 29th Division's commander, Major General Gerhardt, dedicated this site as the Divisional Cemetery. It is five miles southwest of Omaha Beach.

29th Division burials had actually commenced at La Cambe as early as 11 June. The village itself is 1.5 km due East. 29th Division during a dramatic night attack on 7-8th June liberated la Cambe. This was promptly followed-up by their occupation of Isigny after a devastating Allied naval bombardment that left 60 per cent of that town destroyed. One 'Stonewaller' described the town on occupation thus: 'Isigny looked as though somebody had picked it up and dropped it.'

At the dedication ceremony on 23 July a simple signpost marked the site. It was adorned with the division's blue and gray symbol and read:

'This cemetery was established on 11 June 1944 by the 29th Infantry Division who made the supreme sacrifice on the battlefields of Normandy...In command of this valiant legion of the Blue and Gray is Lt. Col. T. Terry, Infantry, who was killed in action 17 July 1944.'

By 23 July the temporary cemetery was already crowded with over 2,000 dead; the white crosses and Stars of David glistened in the Normandy sun, the grass was now trimmed and looked immaculate. The ninety-piece divisional band played mournful music. It was a memorable event as one appointed witness from VII Corps noted:

'It was a very touching ceremony with the dead not yet buried piled up on either side of the honor guard. We were dressed in the cleanest battle uniforms we could find and three people from each Regiment carried guidons.'

The Stonewallers' were removed from La Cambe in 1947 and either repatriated to America at the request of their families, or re-interred at St. Laurent overlooking Omaha Beach.

Today La Cambe is one of the principle 1939-45 German war cemeteries in France. From 1948 onwards the British Graves Registration Service, and then the Commonwealth Wargraves Commission, worked with the French war graves organization to concentrate most of the German dead into six major regional cemeteries. La Cambe now holds the distinction of being the largest German Second World War cemetery in France with 21, 160 burials. The German People's Organization for the Care of War Graves continues to maintain this and all their other cemeteries across Europe. Individual German burials will also be found in several British cemeteries across Normandy; these are original burials conducted by the Graves Registration Service.

When visiting La Cambe, contrast its Teutonic solemnity with the elegant beauty of St. Laurent, or the British Cemetery at Bayeux. Here, the dark stone crosses grouped in five's are purely symbolic. The engraved flat stones mark the actual burials. These show the resting-places of multiple bodies in what the Germans called 'comradeship in death.' In the centre of the cemetery is a prominent grass mound surmounted by a monolithic dark granite cross and two statues representing mourning parents. To the rear of the mound are steps to the top from which the cemetery and surrounding land can be viewed. Be cautious in wet weather, the path and steps can get slippery. Be respectful of this mound; 296 German servicemen lie beneath it.

One burial plot is of particular note. In Block 47, Row 3, Grave

120 lies the remains of SS-Hauptsturmführer Michael Wittmann with two of his Tiger tank crewmen (Rudolf Hirschel and Heinrich Reimers). Wittmann was one of the war's greatest tank aces. He died with his crew between Caen and Falaise on 8 August 1944 during the Canadian Operation Totalise. After the battle his body was placed in an unmarked burial site next to the N158 where it remained until 1983 when the Tiger crew's remains were rediscovered, exhumed and given a proper burial at La Cambe.

If you wish to complete the Visitors Register, examine the cemetery records, or obtain cemetery information and postcards you will need to enter the rooms adjacent to the arched entranceway.

APPENDIX F:

WHERE TO STAY

The Normandy Tourist Board offers an excellent service. The Board can provide lists of recommended hotels, campsites, gîtes and chambre d'hote and having ascertained your preferences will make the booking for you for a small administrative fee. Convenient offices can be found in:

Bayeux: pont St. Jean on the corner between St. Jean and rue Larcher. Tel: 02 31 92 92 40.

Caen: pl. St. Pierre by the Èglise St. Pierre. Tel: 02 31 27 14 14.

Carentan: to the left of the Mairie (Town Hall). Tel: 02 33 42 74 01.

French Government Tourist Offices are located in London and New York:

London: 178 Picadilly, London W1V 0AL. Tel: 0171 629 1272.

New York: 444 Madison Ave., 16th fl., New York, NY 10022. Tel: (212) 439 1400.

INDEX